create three dimensional jewelry

Combine stitching, embellishing, layering, and riveting

Heather DeSimone

create
three
dimensional
jewelry

Combine stitching, embellishing, layering, and riveting

Heather DeSimone

KALMBACH BOOKS

Kalmbach Books
21027 Crossroads Circle
Waukesha, Wisconsin 53186
www.Kalmbach.com/Books

Lettered step-by-step photos by the author and Jess Lovendale Photography. All other photography © 2014 Kalmbach Books.

Published in 2014
18 17 16 15 14   1 2 3 4 5

Manufactured in the United States of America

ISBN: 978-0-87116-494-0
EISBN: 978-1-62700-063-5

Editor: Karin Van Voorhees
Art Director: Lisa Bergman
Photographers: William Zuback and James Forbes

Publisher's Cataloging-In-Publication Data

DeSimone, Heather.
  Create three dimensional jewelry : combine stitching, embellishing, layering, and riveting / Heather DeSimone.

  p. : col. ill. ; cm.

  Issued also as an ebook.
  ISBN: 978-0-87116-494-0

  1. Jewelry making—Handbooks, manuals, etc. 2. Metal-work—Handbooks, manuals, etc.
  3. Beadwork—Handbooks, manuals, etc. I. Title.

TT212 .D47 2014
739.27

contents

introduction

My grandmother used her top bureau drawer to store her jewelry. It was arranged in the various rectangular and square boxes that each piece came in when she bought it—Saks Fifth Avenue boxes sat next to boxes with hen-scratched writing from someone's yard sale reading 10¢. When I was a little girl, I spent hours rearranging her pretties: enameled brooches, knotted glass pearls, a pewter-cast daisy pendant that spun with the words "He loves me" and "He loves me not" on each petal, and my absolute favorite: a necklace made from telephone wire. I trace my love for jewelry to these times, and the time I spent yard sale-ing for old treasures with my great aunt. The past has had an incredible influence on my present jewelry design sensibilities.

my Haskell influence

When I was just starting out as a jewelry designer in my 20s, trying to find my "look," I never felt like my work stood out from the crowd. I was selling at street fairs and craft shows next to many other jewelry makers with very similar aesthetics: freshwater pearls with a sterling-set gemstone pendant in the center; simple drop earrings with cloudy pieces of garnet on sterling silver earring hooks that always matched all the others. My work felt stagnant—even I wasn't inspired by my own creations. Then I discovered the work of Miriam Haskell through Deanna Farneti Cera's book *Costume Jewelry: The Jewels of Miriam Haskell.* This book opened my eyes and provided me with a light-bulb moment—I didn't have to string beads in one direction across my neck. I could *build* my jewelry.

With this insight, I sought to come up with my own aesthetic that used these same techniques of crafting each individual element as well as the overall design. Haskell and her crew commonly, but not solely, used metal or filigree with stacked layers of beads or stitched adornments onto them, as the base of their works. Little did I know that another factor was about to shape my creations. It came in the form of a plastics warehouse.

Miriam Haskell—and her designers including Frank Hess, Robert F. Clark, and others throughout the decades—had the sensibility of craft. Not only did they string elements into delightful necklaces, brooches, *sautoirs*, clip earrings, and more, but the pieces were also crafted with tedious handiwork and attention to detail. Bases of metal filigree were adorned or built with simple stitching techniques, likely borrowed from garment embroiderers and seamstresses of the era. Tiny pavé-set stones or rose montées were used amidst a sea of pearls to create the perfect dash of bling that a statement piece required without going over the top. Clasps were as much a part of the design as centerpieces. Many were more intricately stitched or constructed than the necklace or bracelet itself.

best plastics

In the late spring of 2004, I received an email from a guy named Norm from Rhode Island. He said he had been in the Lucite bead business for a few years and he had some beads to sell.

Along with my mother, Jan Parker, I co-own a company called *The Beadin' Path*. We have sold vintage beads since 1992. We dabbled in vintage Lucite, but back then it was not what most of our customers wanted. At the time, there was a real apprehension in the bead and jewelry components world for anything plastic. In fact, I was a "plastic snob" myself. The email was intriguing, however, and thinking he likely had a shoebox or perhaps even a car trunk full of Lucite beads, I responded to him.

Within two weeks, my mother, my husband, and a few of the fun women who worked for us at the time found ourselves in Pawtucket, R.I., cleaning out a manufacturer's warehouse room the size of two gymnasiums, and loading up three semi-tractor trailer trucks with what eventually equaled 40,000 lbs. of beads, plastic hoops, bangles, and other plastic jewelry-making components. Norm's company had once been the go-to bead maker for the plastic bead industry and had created supplies for companies such as Avon, Coro and Corocraft, Trifari, and others. But, over time, it had shifted its focus away from jewelry making. When the time came to reclaim the long-shut-up-and-dusty warehouse room, it was time to find a buyer for all of the beads, and that was me. Given the amount of beads we had just amassed, I had visions of selling beads as an 80-year-old woman.

So, plastics! I started playing. And as I tried to incorporate the Haskell-inspired techniques I had been developing on my own, a new look to my designs was born. I had been using small, subtle beads built up with lots of sterling silver and other metals to stitch and stack, but now I faced a new challenge: Using these brilliantly bold plastic pieces and inspiring others to use them as well.

how to use this book

This book is divided into three sections. The first section contains the building blocks of dimensional jewelry design. You'll learn all about the materials used in this book, and you'll also learn new ideas to stack, layer, rivet, sew, and more to create elements that can then be incorporated into the jewelry you make. The second section is the heart of the book—the projects. It begins with ideas that add dimension through building out or up, and transitions to ideas that use lashing, stitching, and wrapping to add depth. Finally, at the end of the book you'll find a quickie review of some elementary jewelry-making techniques, such as wrapping loops and crimping strands. The projects use the building block techniques. For some of them, you'll build elements first, such as a stacked flower focal, and then create jewelry using the elements you've just made. Some projects have alternate ideas so you can see how the same technique works with different colors or materials. I've added tips to help you with the mechanics of jewelry making, and tidbits, which are fun facts about style or fashion. I hope you'll learn a lot and have a lot of fun along the way!

Heather DeSimone

Building Blocks are the fundamentals—the techniques that create three-dimensional jewelry. The book begins with detailed instruction that you'll use in the projects later.

element 1

In many projects, you'll build one or more three-dimensional elements and then you'll incorporate them into finished jewelry. Element instructions come first in these projects.

Step-by-step

These instructions are to finish the jewelry using the elements you've just made. I encourage you to be creative here— substitute a chain for a beaded strand, or large beads for small.

alternative project

Often I suggest an alternative idea based on the element introduced in the project. These directions are more general and designed to get your creative ideas flowing.

TIP!

Tips have to do with the specific construction of the jewelry project, in order to make your work go more smoothly.

TIDBIT!

Tidbits are facts about jewelry or fashion that I included for fun. I hope you enjoy them!

disclaimer from a
non-type-A designer

While I dream of time-traveling back to 1930 in New York City and being a fly on the wall looking over the desks of Haskell-house designers Frank Hess and Robert F. Clark, I can only assume what their techniques might have looked like when dissected and broken down into steps.

I am inspired by their finished work, but I have never taken apart a Haskell piece (it wouldn't be the most financially sound decision to make, as these pieces fetch high prices in the collector's market!). So the techniques in this book are my own, inspired by the finished work of these men and their peers.

You should also know a little about my personality and how I work. I love intricate and detailed jewelry; however, I am not the most patient of designers. When I can find a shortcut or quick tip or even hide a boo-boo, I do it.

I have an appreciation for those with a more meticulous approach than mine, but breaking down technique does not come easily to me. I just do it. So, please trust yourself as you try my techniques, and allow yourself to make and leave a few mistakes in your work. Don't get me wrong—I have the utmost respect for craftsmanship and you must make sure your work is sturdy and sound. However, I want you to know that no two surfaces, even with the same two findings, are ever 100-percent identical. As you read my instructions, keep in mind that jewelry in this style is best accomplished with your intuition and your free-thinking interpretations of my approach.

materials

It's natural to want to collect the vintage and classic materials used in early costume jewelry designs if you see them for sale. Ornate metal filigree pieces to use as bases on which to stitch and adorn, mesh clasps, metals, rose montées, nailheads, and other stitchable or sew-on beads such as the teeniest of teeny natural or glass seed pearls beckon, whether you have a design in mind or not. Luckily, many of these components are readily available in today's market as reproduction or newly made pieces. You'll be able to apply the techniques learned in this book to your own personal style, whether it's vintage throwback or über modern.

teensies ▶

I have been collecting what I call *teensies* for years. While I love and use many seed beads, I find it a fun challenge to track down 2–4mm beads in all shapes and finishes. From 2mm silver beads the width of a thread to 3mm gemstones, 2mm vintage glass pearls, and tiny faceted crystal rondelles, collecting teensies is a great way to make sure I have a palette of small beads at my disposal when it's time to create adorned components.

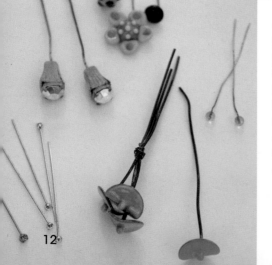

◀ decorative wires and headpins

Headpins and wires embellished with lovely little visual details are a perfect finishing touch for many surfaces of stitched and stacked vintage designs. Aside from the aesthetic purpose of adding detail, these findings also function as anchors and structural devices. Today, Swarovski makes beautiful rose montée-adorned headpins, and Bali and Turkish silver headpins and wires often have additional decoration. Alternatively, look for amazing headpins made by U.S. glass artists and enamelists today, including those by Sylvie Elise Lansdowne (p. 35) and Jennifer Fahnestock.

rose montées, nailheads, and sew-ons ▲

Sew-on beads were used heavily in the stitched work and layered adornment that covered filigrees and other bases in order to build up surface textures. These components are well suited for this type of work because they are flat backed and often offer multiple holes to stitch through. Originally developed in Austria, France, and Czechoslovakia to adorn clothing and textiles, these items are go-to components for beadwork and embellishment.

filigree and ajoure ▲

Filigree components were a standard supply in many of the 1930s–1960s-era pieces that inspired the looks we are creating in this book. It's fortunate that many of the same companies who manufactured pieces for the design houses of those times are still in business, having passed their craft down through generations. These include filigree component manufacturers in Germany and in the U.S.

Today, *filigree* is commonly thought of as any component that has multiple holes, but that definition isn't entirely accurate. Filigree is a component that is made up of fine wires or granulation in a lacing pattern with holes created by negative spaces. Another term, *ajoure*, refers to a blank that has been drilled or a piece of metal that was worked in order to leave holes. We will be working with both types of bases.

custom and unique ▲ filigree and ajoure components

Filigree components are not only made of metals. There are some wonderful Lucite and pressed acrylic pieces available. Components with multiple holes also can be found made from other materials such as wood, plastic, stone, and glass. I'll teach you some simple and fun ways to create your own bases using drilling and punching techniques and unusual materials.

beads and buttons

Beads come in so many shapes and materials. A great majority of the beads in this book are Lucite, but there are plenty of other materials mixed in: shell, gemstone, pearl, crystal, glass, sterling silver, and more. Traditional shapes, such as round and bicone, are plentiful, but we'll also use top-drilled briolette-style beads, pendants, center-drilled beads, shaped beads, washers, and more. You'll learn creative ways to incorporate new shapes as well as standard methods for the more common. *Buttons* are one of my favorites for a closure or clasp. They come in loads of materials and colors so they're easy to match to your beads. Use them as a perfect little finishing accent to the center of a stack of flowers, or string them together like beads for dramatic texture and dimension. Buttons without shanks (with multiple buttonholes), can creatively double as a base, or ajoure, on which you can build up layers of beads and other decoration.

findings and finishings ▶

Clasps, wires, headpins, jump rings, and any other traditional findings are key for stacking and stitching.

We'll use various types of wire in fine gauges. I'm especially fond of 28–30-gauge brass wire because it's stronger, more flexible, and holds its shape better than fine silver wire.

Filigree clasps and screened pieces are resurfacing after virtually disappearing from the jewelry-supplies market for a number of years. These, as well as button earrings and brooches, are a perfect and classic base on which to build stitched and stacked findings and closures.

Chain is another favorite in my bag of tricks. Beyond the traditional use, chain links can become bases on which to build interesting visual elements. Chain is a natural way to accent a stacked or constructed focal piece—just connect it right into the piece with a jump ring or a wire-wrap connection. Always hoard bits of chain as you never know when you might need just a measure of connected metal to finish a piece in the most perfect way.

tools

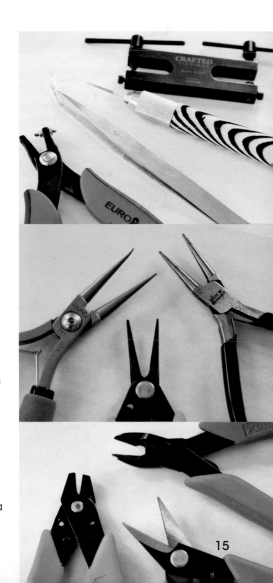

A sharp *awl* is a must-have tool for piercing holes in vinyl, leather, or any fibrous material you might layer in stacks. *Hole-punching pliers* will punch through most light metals and plastics.

As you have already learned, I like shortcuts. I know how to make and set traditional rivets, and I do believe they have their very important place in this world. But for the types of projects featured here, a *riveting tool* does the trick with an ease and speed that you can't get with traditional riveting. My favorite brand (there are a few on the marketplace) is the Crafted Findings Piercing and Riveting tool. It has interchangeable attachments, so you'll only need one tool body, and it can be adjusted to accommodate different rivets and eyelets with different diameters.

My go-to pliers are *roundnose pliers*. With conical, tapered jaws, roundnose pliers are perfect for making loops in many sizes, or turning wire to tighten a stack of beads. My favorites are by Tronex. They're super sturdy, so I can work without worry that the tips will curl or wimp out.

Chainnose pliers have blunt tips and smooth jaws. Use them to stabilize loops when wrapping, or tighten wires during stitching or lashing. My latest joy is Xuron *crimping pliers*. Not only does it make excellent folded crimps, but it has a sweet chainnose on the end. I use it all the time, even when crimps are nowhere to be found.

Sturdy *wire cutters* are critical for the work we'll be doing. For heavier-gauge (24 gauge and thicker) wire cutting, Xuron 9100F cutters have a tapered head that gets into tight spots. The wire retainer keeps snipped ends from flying across the room. You'll also need scissors for finer-gauge wires. The Xuron *high durability scissor* is the only thread or fine wire cutter you will ever want, once you try one. For memory wire, you'll need a pair of Xuron's *hard wire shears*. There is no blade, so it snips or strangles the steel memory wire and "cuts" without ruining your blades.

stacking and working in layers

Layering or stacking is as simple as stringing a series of beads, but you'll be stringing "out" instead of "across." Stack layers from smallest to largest so that each layer is visible from the front of the element. Use different sorts of components to come up with widely varying stacked elements.

how to design in stacks

use center-drilled beads

A common question from my students and customers: "How do you use a bead with a hole in the middle?" If your background is in straight stringing and you haven't yet played with the idea of layering materials and building elements, using a center-drilled bead can be a creative hill to climb.

Don't be afraid to mix and layer varied materials. Try gemstones with metal, stacking Lucite with glass, and so on.

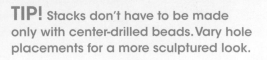

TIP! Stacks don't have to be made only with center-drilled beads. Vary hole placements for a more sculptured look.

how to fix and finish stacks
with wire

what you need
- **3–7** 10mm–35mm assorted center-drilled beads
- **3–5** 6–8mm Lucite baubles
- **2** 4mm spacers
- 5mm jump ring
- 20-gauge wire
- roundnose pliers
- wire cutters

1 Wrap a simple loop on the end of a 6-in. piece of 20-gauge wire. Don't make the wrap too deep as you want it to nestle in the front of the pendant.
2 String a 4mm spacer, the center-drilled beads from smallest to largest, and a 4mm heishi spacer.
3 Make a 90-degree bend and wrap the tail into a button-shank style loop at the top back of the element (see photos).
4 String a few 6–8mm baubles on a jump ring. String the jump ring through the loop on the front of the pendant and close the jump ring.

TIP! A heishi spacer bead provides a clean finish to the front or back of a stack.

with rivets and eyelets

A lovely and clean way to finish stacks is with rivets or eyelets. There are two ways to do this: The traditional method, with a nail set and hammer, and a newer option, with a compression tool.

The Crafted Findings Piercing and Riveting tool is ideal for folks I like to call "kitchen counter metalsmiths"—it's an easy way to make cold connections without a special studio setup. Begin with the flaring wheel for setting eyelets, and then explore other attachments such as those for piercing and for riveting pieces together. The only limit is the diameter and length of the components that work with the tool ($\frac{1}{16}$ and $\frac{3}{32}$ in. diameter and $\frac{1}{16}$ to $\frac{15}{32}$ in. long).

Like I said in my designer disclaimer, I am an instant-gratification, no-muss-no-fuss maker. I find this tool to be the bees knees, and I demonstrate it in a few projects. Please know that if you are a master of traditional riveting, you can feel free to use traditional riveting methods in any of these projects.

traditional set eyelets

what you need
- rubber hammer
- eyelets or rivets
- wooden platform
- nail set and base

1 Place the eyelet on the metal base on a wooden platform.
2 Stack the center-drilled beads together upside down.
3 Insert the nail set and give it a good solid hit with the rubber hammer.
4 Flip the stack over to see a solidly secure eyelet.

—Tips and photos in this section are from jewelry designer Wendy Baker

compression tool set eyelets and rivets

what you need
- Crafted Findings tool
- assortment of rivets and eyelets

eyelets
An eyelet allows many adornment and design opportunities. Eyelets protect wires from fraying or cutting from the rough edges of holes, and they create a finished, smooth look for your piece.

1 Position the eyelet flaring wheel in the tool. Choose the proper-sized eyelet for your stack by trial and error—stack the beads on the eyelet to determine the length that is best. Leave 1/16–1/8 in. extending beyond the stack.

2 Slowly turn the flaring wheel until the eyelet folds over. Use care and caution when determining how tightly to squeeze, as the materials dictate the tension (if you are using soft plastics with metals, you can tighten the eyelet more than if you have layered a harder plastic or another brittle or breakable material in the stack).

3 Remove the element from the tool and admire the smooth-edged eyelet in the center.

rivets
1 Place the blank on the piercing side. Twist the wheel until you feel the tool break through the blank. Don't stop—keep turning the wheel until you can turn no more. This pushes the punched-out metal all the way through. Turn the wheel in reverse until the tool exits the blank.

2 Choose a rivet size based on the depth of the stack. Insert the rivet into the hole and place the stack into the riveting side of the tool with the nail-head side down. Twist the wheel until the rivet splays out and is tight. Don't overtighten. Twist the wheel back. Violà. That's it.

how to adorn stack centers
clusters
Clustering is my favorite way to finish a stacked piece. Simply string a few beads on a headpin and make the first half of a wrapped loop. Connect to the loop at the front of a stack and complete the wraps. Repeat until the cluster is full.

adhering a stone or cabochon
E-6000 is a miracle adhesive that will adhere metals to glass, stone to plastic, or almost any combination of materials. Perch a pointed-back Swarovski crystal in the center of an eyelet, or place a flat-back cabochon over a rivet or headpin and glue in place.

decorative headpins
These are must-haves when you are working in stacks. Find them with crystals, silver or metal tips, or even glass or enamel heads. Use these as both a functional wiring method and a design choice for a finished and fun touch to the centers of stacks.

stitching and creating surface adornment

One of the methods used by Haskell and her designers to create intricate and amazing pieces was stitching and surface adornment. Using mostly metal filigree pieces, they built up decorative layers by stitching strings of tiny glass seed pearls from Japan, rose montées made in Austria and Czechoslovakia, and later, glass beads made in Czechoslovakia and Italy. To me, the material choices distinguish Haskell designs from the others, even today. The techniques, however, can be applied across many materials.

running stitch

what you need

- assorted teensies
- filigree or ajoure base
- 28-gauge wire
- wire cutters

Similar to a running stitch in sewing or embroidery, use this technique when working with fine wire and filigree or ajoure. Stitch with the wire, coming up through the back of the work. Add a bead or two, and stitch back down. Continue until you've added the adornment you desire.

stitching to filigree

what you need

- assorted beads: rose montées, teensies
- filigree, mesh, or ajoure base
- 28-gauge wire
- wire cutters

Start with a simple running stitch, and stitch in a freeform manner up and down and in and out of the holes in the filigree or other base. Make intuitive decisions on where to add extra stitches for security and extra beads and components for visual interest.

 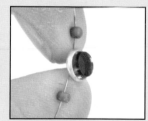  

1 Cut a 2-ft. piece of 28-gauge wire.

2 String a teensie, a rose montée, and a teensie. Leave a 3-in. tail.

3 String each wire end through a hole in the filigree or mesh base, choosing a distance between holes that spans the length of your beaded segment.

4 Weave one wire end through the filigree or mesh base a few times. Repeat with the second wire end.

5 Repeat steps 2 and 3, varying the beads, until the base is adorned to your liking.

6 Finish the end of a wire (when you are finished stitching or when you need to end a wire to add a new one) by sewing the wire through a few nearby stitches. Use flush cutters to trim the end of the wire as close to the stitching as you can, taking care not to clip your stitches.

TIP! Keep the back neat. A big part of keeping the back of your stitched elements smooth and neat is choosing a wire that is soft, flexible, and easy to sew with. Some mesh components come in two pieces so you can snap a setting on the back after you've sewn your embellishments to the front. However, by using the right wire, your tidy stitches won't be a distraction and you will not need an additional setting.

bead wrapping

This technique can be used to create so many amazing variations. Because of my years of digging for vintage bead stock, I happen to know that many of the manufacturers that made glass-coated pearls used from the 1940s–70s pre-strung them on fine-gauge brass wire. We used to find beads by the box and by the pallet all labeled "Made in Japan." It's one of those "If I knew then what I know now" moments, as I wish I had invested in more of those boxes of dainty 2mm pearls on wires. When you examine a vintage piece, you can see why designers preferred the glass pearls to come pre-strung on wires. They could simply then wrap whatever base they wanted to adorn, whether it was a bead, a chain link, a donut-shaped pendant, or a filigree clasp.

what you need
- assorted teensies
- 15mm round bead
- 28-gauge wire
- wire cutters

1 Cut a comfortable length of fine brass wire. String a series of 2–4mm beads.

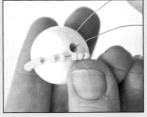

2 Wrap the 15mm bead with the beaded wire.

3 Manipulate where the beads land and turn by shifting the small beads on the wire.

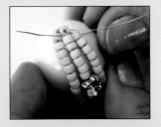

4 To finish the ends of a bead-wrapped element, sew or weave the tail a few times through the last wrap. Neatly trim any extra wire and smooth down any flyaways with rubber-coated pliers.

TIP! If you need to add a new wire, no worries—you haven't underestimated anything. I add wires all the time, and it can be a good thing—a new wire fortifies the element's integrity. Simply cut a comfortable length of wire and make a few stitches through the back of the stitching you've already done. Begin close to where you want to add beads. Bring the wire through to the front, and continue the stitching.

lashing

As beads are added in rows, each new row is *lashed*—or *anchored*—to the previous row. Many well-known designers of the past used a similar technique to coat chain, wire, or components of many shapes with smaller beads. Seed beads and rose montées were common coverage beads back when Haskell, Demario, and Hagler were using the technique. Now you can find tiny crystals, small Czech beads, or tiny gemstones that work equally well.

what you need
- assortment of teensies
- form or component to cover
- loads of 28-gauge brass wire

1 Cut a 2-ft. piece of brass wire. A longer length might make you crazy, and one thing that's great about this technique is that you can add a new wire fairly easily. Anchor the wire to the object you are covering.

2 Estimate the length of coverage you want, and string on the appropriate number of beads. Anchor the first wrap by forming the beads around the base. Reinforce it with a wrap and a knot.

3 Add another row of beads and form it next to the first. Then lash the wire underneath the first anchor wire in the back.

4 Repeat steps 2 and 3, adding or subtracting beads as you need.
5 To finish a lashed piece, simply backlash: Stitch the wire and knot to anchor it under the previous lashing wires. Tie some extra knots and then neatly trim the wires.

One of my favorite Haskell pieces features a bold chain that was created link by pearl-covered link. It's pictured here in Costume Jewelry: The Jewels of Miriam Haskell, *by Deanna Farneti Cera.*

constructing custom components

making chain links

Creating loops with beads and wire and linking them into chain was a common practice that is still effective in modern designs. I have two methods for making chain links from beads: stringing and weaving.

stringing chain links

So simple—create your own chain by stringing a series of beads and knotting them together to create a link. Then repeat, connecting the links as you go.

1 Cut a piece of 26- or 28-gauge wire to three times the length that you want your link to be. String enough beads to reach the length of the link you want. Tie the ends of your wire together using a simple knot.

2 Thread each end of the wire back through a few beads in the link to hide the wire.

3 Trim the wire. Note: Make individual links or thread a new link through the previous one before you knot the ends for a connected chain.

weaving chain links

Peyote stitch is a traditional beadweaving stitch that fits beads together in an offset manner, almost like laying bricks.

1 Cut 3 ft. of 28-gauge wire. You may also use Fireline or a bead weaving thread, if you prefer. Wire gives the links some bend, so they can be almost sculpted one to one another.

2 String an odd number of beads in a length just slightly shorter than the desired circumference of your link.

3 Close the length of beads into a circle by stringing the needle or wire end through the first bead strung in the same direction.

4 Pick up a bead, skip the next bead, and string the wire through the third bead in the ring, locking the newly added bead into place. Repeat until you have circled the entire ring. String the wire through the last bead in the original ring.

5 Pick up a bead and string the wire through the first bead in the previous round. Pick up a bead, skip the next bead, and string the wire through the next bead. Repeat to create as many rows as you need to make the link as thick or narrow as you like.

6 When you are finished, weave the working wire through several beads in the body of the weaving to secure, and then trim any excess wire.

making cluster cuties

One of my favorite custom-built techniques creates a little hand-made element I refer to as a *cutie*. Please use your own instincts and make your own decisions about which size beads to use, depending on the look you want to achieve. This is a very flexible technique!

Cuties are created with ladder stitch, commonly used in seed bead weaving. Be sure the holes in your beads are large enough to pass 26–28-gauge wire through 2–4 times.

what you need
- **8** 6x9mm top-drilled drop beads
- **4** 4–6mm sew-on or disk beads
- **12** in. 26–28-gauge brass wire

tools
Xuron precision scissors

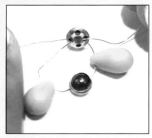

1 Cut a 12-in. piece of wire. String one drop, one sew-on, one drop, and one sew-on. Form a circle with the beads by passing the wire tail through the sew-on. Pull tight.

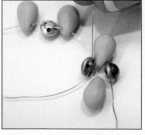

2 Pick up one drop, one sew-on, and one drop. String the wire through the second sew-on in the cluster created in 1. Pull tight.

3 Repeat step 2.

4 Pick up one drop, one sew-on, and one drop. Pass one wire end back through the hole in the first sew-on. Pass the other end of the wire through the same sew-on in the opposite direction.
5 Pull the wires to form a rounded cluster, or Cutie.

6 Reinforce the Cutie by using the wire on each end to stitch through the teardrop holes only, on each end. Pull tight to reinforce the shape.
7 Tie an overhand knot on each end, under an anchored piece of wire. Trim each end carefully.

making bases or custom ajoure

Almost anything—*anything*—can be made into an ajoure-style base for a jewelry element. Whether it's a piece of metal from an old sentimental keychain or a plastic doll part, with just a few essential tools, you can make these surfaces into something that is easily adorned. Use a rotary tool with a regular jewelers drill bit to make holes in Lucite. Want to do the same with glass or stone or shell? No problem, just switch the bit to a diamond-tipped one. Making a base with a soft material such as leather or vinyl? Use an awl. Whatever you want to make into a base, there's almost always a way to do so.

begin with a drilling station

A drilling set up **A** is an amazing addition to your jewelry studio. You can create beads, components, and bases out of almost anything using one. What do you need?

a low dish with water: A casserole dish or small pan works great. It has to be low enough that you can see well into it and deep enough to cover your base and piece you're drilling. Drilling underwater keeps the drill bit from overheating.

block of wood base: Small enough to be submerged under water in your dish **B**, but big enough to act as a base to fit the piece you're drilling.

a Dremel tool: Almost any lightweight drill will work.

a collet adapter: Generally the collet that comes with the Dremel is too wide for a jewelry-sized bit.

jewelry drill bits: Regular bits for soft materials including wood, Lucite, and plastics, and diamond-coated bits for stones, glass, shell, and other hard materials.

safety gear: Wear eye protection and a mask, just in case. Even though the water grabs any would-be airborne dust particles, some shell, when inhaled, can be lethal. Err on the side of caution.

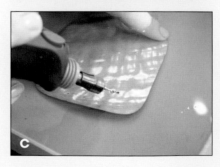

make a base out of glass or shell

what you need
- piece of glass or shell
- drilling station with diamond-coated bit, eye protection and mask

Hold the item to be drilled under water against the wood block. Position the drill bit where you'd like the hole and drill **C**. Turn the drill off and remove from the water.

make a base out of Lucite or plastic

what you need
- piece of Lucite or plastic
- drilling station with jewelers drill bit

Use the same technique as for glass and shell, but instead of using a diamond-tipped drill bit, switch to a plain jewelry bit **D**. The diamond tips will just get clogged up with melted plastic. You want a smooth bit to drill plastic.

make a base out of leather or vinyl

what you need
- leather or vinyl shape
- beading awl

TIP! Use a compression setter or the Crafted Findings tool to set eyelets into metal bases. This creates a smooth and finished hole which you can then adorn or stitch to without worry that the raw metal will wear down or break your wire.

1 Mark the desired locations of the holes on the leather or vinyl. Use a beading awl and twist, applying pressure, to pierce the hole. Be careful where you place your hand—awls are sharp!
2 Alternatively, use a hole-punching tool.

make a base out of metal

what you need
- metal hole punch or the Crafted Findings tool

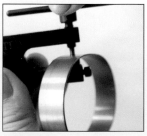

TIP! Use hammers to make different textures on metal blanks. Or use metal stamps to make text or other motif-oriented designs on metal bases.

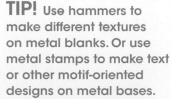

1 Mark the desired location of the holes on the metal. Using the hole punch or riveting tool, pierce the metal hole.
2 The Crafted Findings tool leaves very smooth holes. If you have some burrs left from your punch, use a file to smooth edges so your wire doesn't get cut while you're stitching.

reclaiming vintage jewelry and findings

A vintage jewelry lover's disclaimer: I have a thing about repurposing jewelry. While I love the look of old items used in new pieces, I can only justify reworking or breaking apart vintage goods if there is damage to the piece and the repurposing will makes it usable again. Here are a few things to look for before you dissect old jewelry:

Signatures: It's not always economically wise to rework signed jewelry. Look the name up online. Even if it's not valuable today, it may be someday.

Signature looks: Many of Haskell's pieces were not signed, specifically the earlier and most valuable pieces. If you are not familiar with vintage designer jewelry, show your piece to someone who is before you make the decision to dismantle it.

Easy repairs: Even repaired vintage jewelry has both intrinsic value and historical value. Jewelry designers today wouldn't know nearly as much about design or construction if it wasn't for the catalog of vintage jewelry available to us. With that said, here are some questions to ask before you repurpose:

Will it improve the look?
Will it make me more likely to wear it, give it as a gift, or sell it so that it gets enjoyed?
Does it need repair? Would someone else simply donate it or throw it away?

If you answered yes to any of these questions, please upcycle, reclaim, and adapt away, with my blessing. Here is how:

cleaning

Hold the piece face up and use a dry toothbrush to lightly brush the front to dislodge any dust or dirt. Glue or rewire any loose parts. Loose rhinestones? Use a pin to push the stone out, apply fresh glue, and replace the stone. Old glue breaks down over time, so this is a preventative measure. Lost rhinestones? Glue a spare into the divots that remain. There is no hard rule that says you have to use the same colored stones as replacements, so mix it up.

If there is a chip in an enamel finished piece, make a quick repair with a coat of colored or clear enamel nail polish. Spray lacquer provides an even and protective finish for the surface.

removing backings from earrings and pins

You'll find that there are different types of backings on old-style earrings, pins, and brooches.

harp hinge clip-on earrings

Use flatnose or chainnose pliers to pull off the clip at the hinge. No cutting should be required. Use the same pliers to bend the join up. There should be two remaining holes. Add jump rings to the holes and they become a pendant or charm.

simple style clip-on earrings

For this style clip, pull off the clip at the hinge. If there is no hinge, cut off the clip with wire cutters, leaving a piece of leftover metal still attached to the earring. Use roundnose pliers to make a loop with the remaining metal and then add a jump ring.

screwback earrings

Most screwbacks are either riveted or attached with adhesive to their earring. Clip off the threaded screw attachment finding, leaving enough wire to roll a loop using roundnose pliers. Attach a jump ring and the new charm is ready.

pins and brooches

Vintage pins can be found in various styles and are attached to their findings in different ways. If the pin is riveted, snip the finding off on either side of the rivet, making sure not to disturb the point where it is attached to the brooch. If it's glued on, use a cleanser such as Goof Off and brush on just around the finding, so that you don't harm any enamel or paint on the piece itself. If the finding is cast or just a part of the pin itself, use good cutters and then file any loose or sharp metal that might be left over. Once the pin finding is removed, use a drill or piercing tool to pierce a hole, or add jump rings to any remaining hardware.

reviving old chains

The chain used in older costume jewelry is usually a really high-quality treasure to find. In most cases, you can save and reuse old pieces of chain in varying lengths, simply by cleaning it and pulling off any findings on the ends. If you are working on a mesh or snake chain that is not made with links, you may want to remove clasps, but keep connection hardware in place.

projects

stacked
pendant
earrings

This project can be made with countless variations of materials to achieve different looks. The overall idea is to practice designing using stacks. Experiment with various-sized flat components and beads. Look especially for pieces that have center holes, but not exclusively. In most of these examples, stack from smallest to largest, front to back.

materials

- **2** 50mm center-drilled Lucite or plastic disks
- **2** 30mm center-drilled metal flower components
- **2** 10mm center-drilled Lucite flower components
- **2** 6mm sequins
- **4** 4mm crystal bicones
- **2** decorative headpins
- pair of earring wires

tools

- roundnose pliers
- wire cutters

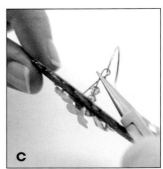

Step-by-step

1 On a headpin, stack a sequin, flower components from smallest to largest, and a Lucite disk **A**.

2 Make a 90-degree bend in the headpin **B**.

3 String two 4mm bicones. Make the first half of a wire-wrapped loop, string the loop of an earring wire **C**, and complete the wrapped loop.

4 Make a second earring.

TIP! Use the Crafted Findings tool and an eyelet to secure the stack from the sequin to the largest component. It's not necessary, but it helps keep the stack together in a clean way.

TIP! Using a larger gauge headpin helps to strengthen the tightness of the earring and the stack.

materials

- **2** 20mm center-drilled metal disks
- **2** 12x25mm center-drilled metal leaf components
- **2** 8mm heishi or washer beads
- **2** ⅙-in. eyelets
- **2** 8mm oval jump rings
- **2** 3mm round jump rings
- pair of earring wires

tools

- Crafted Findings tool
- **2** pairs of pliers
- hole punch pliers
- wire cutters

Step-by-step

1 Layer a heishi, a metal disk, and a leaf component.

2 Attach the layers with an eyelet and the Crafted Findings tool.

3 Punch a hole in the top of the leaf component.

4 Connect an oval jump ring to the stack. Use a 3mm jump ring to attach the earring wire to the oval jump ring.

5 Make a second earring.

button
earrings

The button-shaped earring is a classic. It's the design that comes to mind, for me, if someone says "vintage earrings." Back then, button earrings had clip-on or screwback findings, as pierced ears were uncommon. This update uses pierced earring findings (but make yours clip-ons if you prefer). Using the stacking technique found in building blocks (p. 16), you'll learn how to alter the look of your earrings by varying the sizes and shapes in the layers.

materials

- **2** 40mm center-drilled flowers
- **2** 12mm cup-shaped beads
- **2** 6mm flat heishi pearls or beads
- **2** 4mm washers, spacers, or heishi beads
- **2** decorative headpins
- pair of glue-on post earring findings with backs
- E6000 adhesive or Gorilla Glue

tools

- roundnose pliers
- wire cutters
- Xuron precision scissors

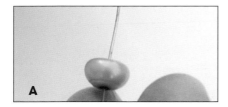

Step-by-step

1 Stack a 6mm flat heishi onto a decorative headpin **A**, followed by a cup-shaped bead and large flower, or base, bead **B**.

2 Add a flat brass spacer or heishi bead **C**.

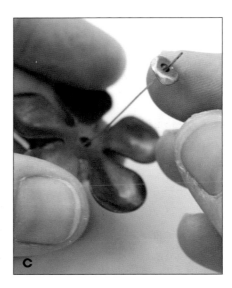

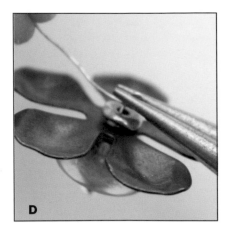

3 Using roundnose pliers, roll a tight loop on the back behind the brass heishi bead **E**. Wrap the wire around the loop, using the wrapping to tighten the stack as you go. Trim off excess wire from the headpin.

4 Using glue, adhere a post earring finding to the back of a petal **F**.

5 Make a second earring.

alternative project: button centerpiece

materials
- **2** buttons with metal loop shanks
- **2** 40mm soft plastic filigree components
- pair of glue-on post earring findings with backs
- E-6000 adhesive or Gorilla Glue

tools
- wire cutters
- Xuron precision scissors

1 Apply a very small amount of adhesive to the back of the button, but not to the shank.

2 Push the shank through the hole in the soft plastic filigree. This should be something you can do easily, but if the shank is larger than the hole in your component, use roundnose pliers to stretch the hole. Let the glue dry.

3 Use adhesive to attach the post earring component to the back of the filigree.

4 Repeat to make a second earring.

alternative project: flower pot brooch

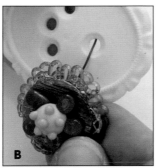

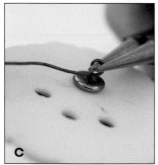

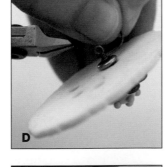

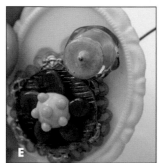

materials

- **2–3** center-drilled washers, filigree bases, or beads in several sizes
- **5–7** small center-drilled flower or disk beads
- ajoure base
- **4** decorative headpins
- 4mm heishi or spacer bead

tools

- roundnose pliers
- wire cutters

1 Thread a decorative headpin (this one is by Sylvie Elise Lansdowne) through the copper washer, brass filigree, and Lucite filigree components **A**. String the stack through the ajoure resin base using the middle hole **B**. String a brass heishi washer.

2 Using roundnose pliers, make a wire-wrapped loop against the brass heishi bead, using the wrapping to tighten and strengthen the stack in front of the ajoure piece **C**. Trim any extra wire **D**.

3 Repeat steps 1 and 2 using smaller components to create the "flowers" in your pot **E, F**. Finish each stack on the back of the ajoure base the same way.

4 Using adhesive, set a pin finding onto the back of the brooch and allow to dry thoroughly.

boat seats to begonias
statement necklace

When we discovered some overstock vinyl at a local fabric warehouse, Ashley's Bunting's wheels were spinning. She envisioned and then helped create a line of upcycled vinyl flowers that could be worked into jewelry of all kinds. In this project, you'll work with intermixing vinyl flowers with metal, Lucite flowers, and other materials. Be inspired to use and combine other fabrics and fibers along with your beads.

materials

- **5** 75–80mm vinyl flowers (large)
- **3** 60mm vinyl flowers (medium)
- **4–7** 25–30mm metal flower components with center hole
- **5–7** 10–25mm metal or Lucite flower components, or metal disks with center hole
- **12mm** cup-shaped bead
- **1–5** 6mm beads
- **3** 4mm bicone crystals
- **5** 4mm washer or heishi beads
- **5** 20-gauge headpins
- **15** sturdy 6mm jump rings
- **1 ft.** chain
- clasp

tools

- roundnose pliers
- chainnose pliers
- wire cutters
- awl

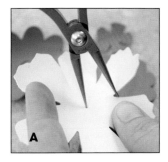
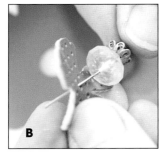

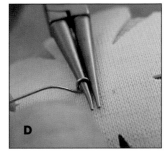

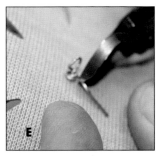

⊖lement layered flower

1 Pierce a hole in the center of each vinyl flower using an awl or the tip of roundnose pliers **A**.

2 Make a stack on a headpin beginning with a 4 or 6mm bead and adding flowers or disks in order from smallest to largest. End with a large vinyl flower and a 4mm washer **B, C**.

3 Use roundnose pliers to roll a loop on the back of the flower element. The loop doesn't need to be functional, but it serves as a tightening mechanism to firm up your stacked flower. Trim the wire tail **D, E**.

4 Repeat steps 2 and 3 to make four additional flowers, varying the order or the components as you'd like.

5 Optional: Make a cluster (Building Block, p. 18) at the front of a component **F**.

⊖tep-by-step

1 Put the flower elements on your workspace and decide the placement for the necklace. Use the awl to pierce holes on each side of each element. Place the holes on the upper sides, not in the middle.

2 Turn the flowers face down. Use the jump rings to attach the chain to the flowers using the holes on each side and the loop in the center. Pay attention to how the elements lay next to each other—there needs to be a U-shaped curve to the front of the necklace, not a straight line.

3 Use a jump ring to attach the clasp to one chain end. Attach a jump ring to the other chain end.

live·life·love
pendant necklace

My son Maximus made this love pendant for me when he was seven. He enjoys hammering metals including brass and copper and he stamps funny words on them from time to time. I first taught him how to do stamping and light metalwork when he was six. My favorite part of this pendant is that he wasn't concerned with how straight the letters were, and that the hammering wasn't perfect, yet it has such a fine quality to it. So I used it in this collaborative piece. This design is a good example of very simply stacked piece and how you can alternate materials.

materials

- 30mm Lucite snowflake wheel
- leaf or oval brass blank
- 25mm metal brass round blank
- 10mm brass washer or round blank
- eyelet sized for width of stack, approx. ⅛ in.
- 24 in. brass chain
- **2** 5mm jump rings
- clasp

tools

- roundnose pliers
- nylon-jaw pliers
- wire cutters
- chasing hammer
- stamping hammer
- riveting tool and vise
- letter stamps
- bench block
- permanent marker
- metal polishing pad
- Crafted Findings tool

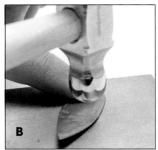

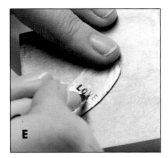

⊖lement 1 leaf pendant

1 Use roundnose or nylon-jaw pliers to straighten out the brass leaf component so it's smooth enough to hammer **A**.

2 Use a chasing hammer to pound down the wavy edges, adding texture as you go, until you have the desired mottled look to your leaf **B**.

3 Use the marker to mark dots where you want your letters to be. For example, if you want the word LOVE, mark four dots to indicate where you will stamp. Be sure to take into account the width of your stamps **C**.

4 Stamp the letters onto the dots, using swift and steady hammering **D**.

5 To darken the letters, color in with the marker **E**, and then polish away any excess black with the polishing pad **F**.

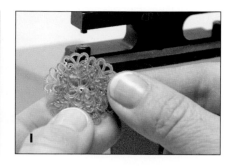

Element 2 riveted wheel

1 Mark the center of the round brass blank. Mark where you desire the words to be. Repeat steps 3 and 4 of element 1 to stamp the letters. Darken and polish as in step 5 of element 1.

2 Use either the piercing side of the riveting tool or a metal hole punch to pierce the center of the blank.

3 Stack the Lucite snowflake wheel, the stamped round blank you just completed, and a washer. Insert a rivet or eyelet (making sure to change your fly wheel over on your tool to the appropriate adapter) **G**.

4 Set the eyelet using the eyelet adapter side of the tool **H**. When working with the eyelets and Lucite is a part of the mix, be sure to tighten the eyelet so it's solid, but not too tight so that it pokes through the holes **I**.

Step-by-step

1 Use a jump ring to connect the leaf pendant and the stacked wheel element. Close securely **A**.

2 Add another jump ring to the top of the pendant at the wheel. (You should be able to string it through one of the holes in the Lucite piece.) Attach the chain and finish with clasp.

alternative project: kinetic pendant

This project shows how stacking and layering can be used to construct components that have functionality. Inspired by my Grandmother's "He Loves Me, He Loves me Not" daisy necklace I found when I used to sort her jewelry as a little girl, this piece shows how one can create a movable pendant with petals that can slide.

stacked
ring

Make an intensely fabulous ring using a crazy-simple technique. By stacking layers of center-drilled pieces, you can create a dynamic component that is perfect for the starring role in a cocktail ring. We'll do a quick bit of stacking and stitching in this ring, as well as pierce a hole in a metal ring blank.

materials

- 35mm round filigree
- **3** metal blanks or pieces with center holes in graduated sizes
- 6–8mm side drilled glass or Lucite bead
- 3–5mm washer or heishi bead
- ring blank or base
- 18 in. 28-gauge brass wire

tools

- Crafted Findings tool or Metal Hole Punch (optional)

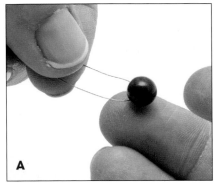

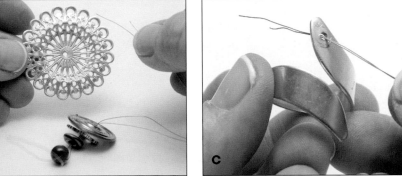

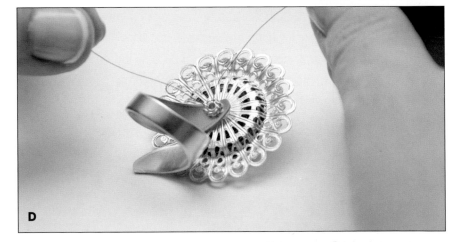

TIP! Two wires are always better than one. Just like in embroidery with fibers and threads, you want to reinforce your knots anywhere you can hide them.

Step-by-step

1 Loosely fold the wire in half. String the side-drilled bead and center on the wire at the fold **A**.

2 Over both wire ends, string the center hole of each of the three graduated pieces from smallest to largest. String the filigree **B**.

3 String both ends through the ring base **C**. (Pierce a hole if needed.)

4 String both ends through the heishi or washer bead **D**.

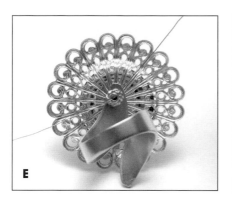 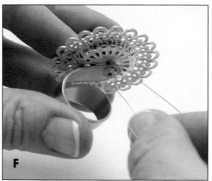 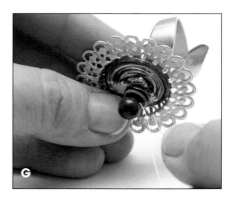

5 Separate the wire ends and wrap each one tightly between the washer bead and the ring base. Reinforce with an overhand knot and pull tight **E, F**.

6 If your ends are long enough, string the wires back up through the ring and repeat the wrap to reinforce. Make a knot between another set of components **G**.

7 Neatly trim any extra wire.

alternative projects: flat-front rings

VINTAGE TIDBIT! Cocktail rings were especially trendy during the days of prohibition. Rebellious fashionistas would wear these large and eye-catching rings to flaunt the fact that they were classy and indulging in some spirits.

Get a sleeker look by fixing the stack with an eyelet or rivet instead of wiring the stacks to the ring base.

and a bold bracelet

Use the same techniques as the stacked ring project, only on a larger scale, to create a cuff bracelet. Add little baubles or charms to the center using the clustering technique taught in "how to adorn stack centers" (p. 18).

memory wire
cuff

This bracelet combines a few building block techniques but leaves loads of room for creative expression. You can really vary the outcome based on the materials you use. From garnets and silver to vintage Lucite and old filigree, this bracelet can bridge the gap between fine jewelry and gypsy style. Use riveting, stacking, and basic bracelet construction in this versatile project.

element 1 the stacked focal

1 String a 4mm bead on a headpin. String a corner of the filigree component from front to back. String a 4mm bead and make a tight wrapped loop **A, B**.

3 Repeat step 2 at the remaining corners and the middle of each side **C**.

4 Layer the flat components on the filigree from largest to smallest and place a rivet through the center **D**. Use the riveting tool to close the eyelet, taking care not to overtighten, especially if you use glass as shown.

materials (filigree bracelets)
- 50–60mm filigree component
- **1–3** additional center-hole flat components in graduated sizes
- **8** 20-gauge headpins
- **12** 4mm round beads
- assorted round and rondelle beads and bead caps
- eyelet sized to fit stack
- **3** memory wire coils

tools
- needlenose pliers
- roundnose pliers
- memory wire cutters
- Crafted Findings tool

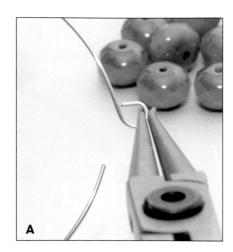

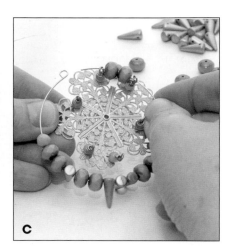

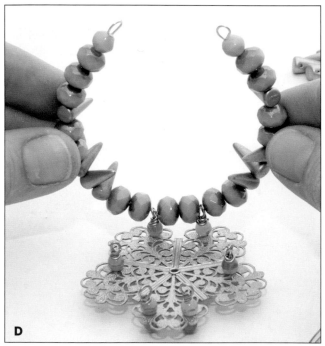

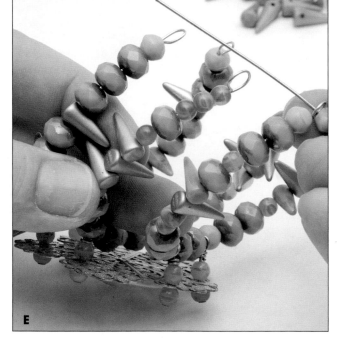

Step-by-step

1 Make a loop at one end of a memory wire coil **A**.

2 String beads in any order until you are almost at the midpoint.

3 String a corner loop from the filigree unit, enough beads to span the back of the filigree, and another corner loop **B, C**.

4 String beads until the end of the coil. Make a loop with the wire end **D**.

5 Repeat steps 1–4 with another coil, connecting the loops at the center of the filigree. Repeat steps 1–4 with the third coil, connecting the loops at the remaining corners of the filigree.

6 String one or two beads on a headpin. String the loop at the end of the first memory wire coil **E**, a few more beads, the loop at the end of the middle memory wire coil, a few more beads, the loop at the end of the remaining memory wire coil, and one or two more beads. Make a loop at the end of the headpin.

7 Repeat step 6 on the other end of the bracelet.

materials (silver and garnet bracelet)

- 20x35mm silver oval component
- 3–5mm bead assortment for focal
- **150** 4mm silver or metal beads
- **6–8** 15mm two-hole spacer bars or beads
- **6** 10mm flat disk beads
- **3** memory wire coils
- **8** 11º seed beads
- **8** heishi or washer beads
- **8** 22-gauge headpins, sterling silver
- **2** ft. 28-gauge fine silver wire
- Gorilla Glue

tools

- Crafted Findings tool
- Xuron precision scissors
- Xuron tweezer nose pliers

TIP! Having a hard time getting your wires tight? The Xuron tweezer nose pliers #450 is tiny enough at the tips to get into some really small crevices and it won't break the wire.

Element 1
the oval focal

1 Picturing a clock face, use a marker and make a dot at the 12, 3, 6, and 9 positions. Add three dots between each set, being sure that facing dots are aligned. Use the piercing side of the tool to make 1/16-in. holes **A**.

2 String an 11º seed bead on a headpin. String it through the hole at "12 o'clock" from front to back. Repeat on either side.

3 Repeat step 2 at the "6 o'clock" position.

4 String an 11º on a headpin and string it through the hole at "3 o'clock." Repeat at "9 o'clock."

5 On each headpin, string a washer or heishi and make a sturdy wrapped loop.

6 Fold the 28-gauge wire in half loosely. String one end through the hole at "3 o'clock" and pull through to the halfway point. String enough beads to span the width and exit through the hole at "9 o'clock." String one wire end from back to front at the next hole (moving toward "12 o'clock" and the other end from back to front at the adjacent hole moving toward "6 o'clock." Add beads, stretch the wire across the focal, and exit through the next open hole. Repeat until you've covered the oval with nine rows of beads. Anchor your wires when you are finished with a lash and a knot, and then trim neatly.

Step-by-step

1 Dab glue at one end of a memory wire coil. Adhere a 10mm disk bead. Allow the glue to set.

2 On the memory wire coil, string a few silver beads, a two-holed bead or spacer bar, several more silver beads and another bar. String silver beads until you are almost to the center of the memory wire.

3 String the first of the "12 o'clock" loops in your oval element. String a silver bead, and the second loop. String a silver bead and the third loop.

4 String beads and spacers in the opposite order of step 2.

5 Repeat step 1 at the wire end.

6 Repeat steps 1 and 2 with a second memory-wire coil, picking up the second hole of the spacers from step 2 as you reach them.

7 When you get to the oval feature, string the first side loop, silver beads to span the back of the oval, and the second side loop. String beads to complete the second half of coil 2, making sure to pick up the two-holed spacers from coil 1 as you go.

8 Repeat step 1 to end the coil.

9 Repeat steps 1–5 with the third memory wire coil, passing through the loop at the "6 o'clock" position.

stacked garden
statement necklace

This necklace incorporates stacked elements made using the Crafted Findings tool. You can also use traditional rivets or even headpins and wire to create these components and achieve the same look. Once your flowers are made, it's just a few more steps to link your bouquet into a stunning collar.

materials

- **9** 25mm Lucite snowflake components
- **3** 18mm center-hole metal disks
- **4** 10–40mm center-hole metal flowers
- **4** 8–20mm Lucite or soft acrylic center-hole flower beads
- 10mm center-hole metal disk
- **9** $^3/_{16}$-in. diameter brass eyelets measuring about $^1/_8$ in. long
- 12 in. chain
- **10** 6mm jump rings
- **2** 4mm jump rings
- clasp

tools

- chasing hammer
- Crafted Findings tool
- vise
- bench block
- chainnose pliers

⊖lement the stacked components

1 Layer one or two metal components or flowers on a snowflake.

2 Insert a $^3/_{16}$-in. eyelet through the center holes. If it doesn't go through easily, use the Crafted Findings tool to stretch the center holes. Or, use very fine roundnose pliers or a metal hole punch with a $^3/_{16}$-in. diameter punch.

3 Using the Crafted Findings tool, insert the stacked component into the riveting/eyelet flaring side of the tool **A**. Flare the eyelet, making sure the tension is tight, but not tight enough to squish or dent any of the components **B**.

4 Repeat to make a total of nine components. Vary your designs or keep them the same.

⊖tep-by-step

1 Connect the components with 6mm jump rings **A**.

TIP! Make sure to connect the snowflakes about one-third of the way on the circle, not right in the middle. This will help the necklace to curve naturally around your neck and also lie flat.

2 Connect a chain end to an end of the focal piece with a jump ring. Repeat on the other side.

3 Cut the chain in half. Use 4mm jump rings to attach a clasp half to each end.

riveting
bangle bracelets

From layered flowers to polka-dotted disks and vintage lockets, this bangle project offers versatility of style. Adorn any metal bracelet using this technique. Stack them together for a clustered look or wear one special piece as a stand-alone statement. Practice using the riveting tool in this project and work with eyelets and stacking components of your choice. Take your stacks to the next level with some sewn-on adornments.

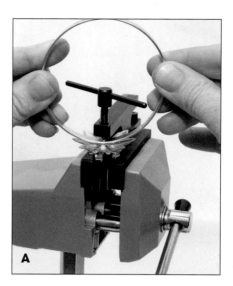

materials

bangle 1: locket bangle
- 10mm bangle blank
- **5** metal shapes
- locket
- **6** ³⁄₃₂-in. Crafted Findings eyelets

bangle 2: stacked garden bangle
- 10mm bangle blank
- **6** 25mm metal flowers with center hole
- **6** 20mm metal flowers with center hole
- **6** 10–15mm metal flowers with center hole
- **6** ³⁄₃₂-in. Crafted Findings eyelets

bangle 3: coin bangle
- 10mm bangle blank
- **6** 20mm torched and textured copper disks
- **6** ³⁄₃₂-in. Crafted Findings eyelets

bangle 4: knotted heart bangle
- 10mm bangle blank
- **6** metal heart blanks
- **6** 12mm knot components
- 2–3 ft. 28-gauge brass wire
- **6** ³⁄₃₂-in. Crafted Findings eyelets

tools
- Crafted Findings tool with ³⁄₃₂-in. piercing attachment, ³⁄₃₂-in. eyelet attachment, and ³⁄₃₂-in. eyelet dome base
- dome base and hammer
- fine-tip permanent marker

Step-by-step
bangles 1, 2, and 3

1 Mark the position of each embellishment on the blank, keeping the marks evenly spaced.

2 Using the Crafted Findings tool, make sure the domed base is in place, and pierce a hole in the blank on each dot.

3 Stack the flowers, disks, or shapes from large to small (on an eyelet and pull the eyelet through the bangle.

4 Set the stack including the bangle into the riveting tool and set the eyelet, finishing off the eyelet on the front. Use light tension if you want your pieces to spin **A, B**.

5 Repeat steps 3 and 4 until all six elements are set on the bracelet.

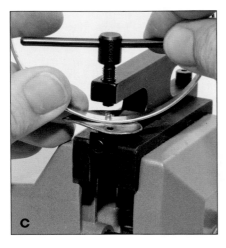

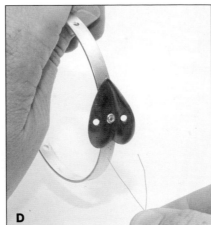

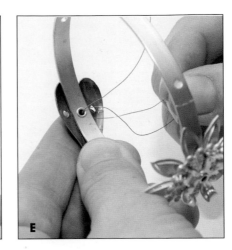

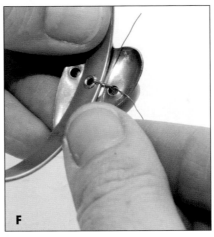

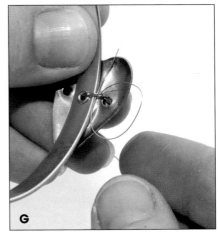

bangle 4

1 Set a knot element on a heart blank. Using a fine-tip marker, mark dots on the heart on the outer sides of the knot. Remove the knot and use the ⅟₁₆-in. piercing wheel to make holes in the heart blank as marked. Repeat for all the hearts.

2 Use a dome block and hammer and put a slight curve into the heart blanks so they match the curve of the bangle.

3 Use a marker to make dots on the bangle and the heart blank where the center of each heart will attach to the bangle. Use the ³⁄₃₂-in. piercing attachment to pierce holes in the heart blanks and the bangle. Put the bangle into the tool so the curve of the bangle matches the domed base.

4 Using the ³⁄₃₂-in. eyelet attachment, set the heart blanks to the bangle bracelet **C**.

5 Cut a 12-in. piece of wire. String a knot element to the center of the wire. Stitch one end of the wire through the eyelet on the heart **D** and the other end through one of the smaller holes in the heart.

With this working end, stitch back up through the eyelet **E**, over the knot, and down through the hole. Repeat to secure the knot.

Repeat the process with the other wire end on the other half of the heart. Finish with a few lashes and knots to secure **F, G,** and then trim neatly.

6 Repeat step 5 until all knots are wired onto the bangle.

TIP! If you aren't able to find the same blanks or knots, there are many other components that can be substituted.

fly away
wrap bracelet

I am beyond-in-love with the wrap bracelet phenomenon. Thanks to designer Chan Luu, a new medium for bracelets has been unearthed. By combining leather with…anything…you can make a gritty and earthy piece that is also sophisticated and refined. This is my twist on a wraparound with some stacked-and-riveted elements. Create almost any look you love by changing the materials. Whether it's handwrapped glass, layered vintage Swarovski crystal with gold-plated metals, or whatever has captured your heart at the moment, make this style your own.

materials

- 10x12mm brass butterfly stamping
- glass cabochon
- 18 in. 10mm wide leather
- 12–15 Swarovski filigree flowers
- **9** 10mm copper caps or rondelles
- 2 in. chain
- swivel lobster claw clasp
- **18** ³⁄₃₂-in. Crafted Findings eyelets
- E6000 adhesive

tools

- Crafted Findings tool with ³⁄₃₂-in. piercing attachment and ³⁄₃₂-in. eyelet setting attachment
- permanent marker

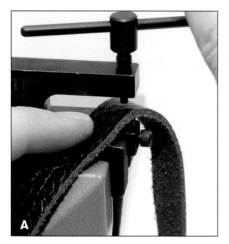

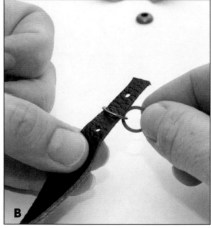

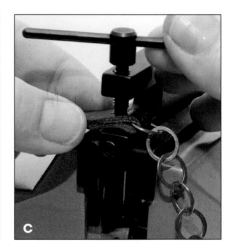

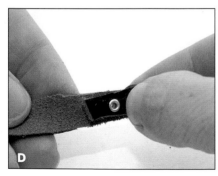

Step-by-step

1 String one end of the leather strap through the end link of chain. Mark the position for the eyelet on each side. Remove the leather. Using the Crafted Findings tool, pierce two holes in the leather **A**. It's easiest to do each hole separately so your leather gets pierced cleanly.

2 String the end of the leather through the chain link **B,** fold the leather end under, and set the first eyelet through the two holes **C, D**.

3 Mark the position of the flowers and cap components, making sure to leave space for the butterfly. The wrap lines up well if you follow this pattern: 1 in. of space; set the first flower. Mark a dot for 12 elements every ¾ in. Leave 2 in. open for the butterfly, then continue with marks for four more elements, ¾ in. apart. Set all of the components using eyelets **E**, **F**, **G**.

4 Repeat steps 1 and 2 on the other end of the leather, substituting the swivel lobster claw clasp for the chain **H**.

5 Pierce a hole through the body of the butterfly component. Set it to the leather in the space reserved with the eyelet setting attachment. Using glue, adhere the glass cabochon on top of the eyelet in the butterfly's body. Dry for 24 hours.

TIP! Use copper caps underneath the smaller Swarovski flower components to give some extra height.

captain
sea star
necklace

I have a fun collection of old military trims and bullion. It's all metallic but it's dark and industrial looking. It adds some glitz, but it's dirty glitz. I love using it as a cording or base for a necklace or bracelet, especially when I have some sort of sculptured focal pieces to add. It can act as a very sturdy anchor for things, such as these sculpted pearl stars.

materials

- **12** freshwater stick pearls, drilled at the tips, 1 in. or longer
- **2** 10mm center drilled glass flowers or rondelles
- **2** 1-in. or larger diameter two-hole buttons
- **2** Czech glass spike beads
- **2** flat center-holed filigrees or metal pieces
- 24 in. military bullion cording
- 24 in. antique brass trim or ribbon
- **2** 12-in. pieces of 22-gauge wire
- **2** shell ovals or donuts
- **36–48** in. of fine brass wire
- toggle half of a clasp
- heavy-duty tape

tools

- wire cutters
- Xuron precision scissors

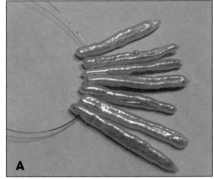

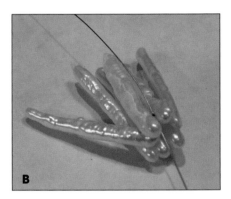

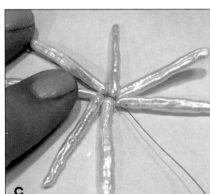

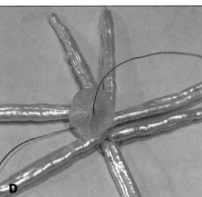

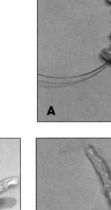

⊖lement 1 the stars

1 Cut a 24–30-in. piece of fine brass wire. String seven freshwater pearls to the center of the wire **A**. String the wire tail back through the beads in the same direction **B** and pull snug to create a circle of wire with the pearls spreading out to look like a seven-pointed star **C**. Repeat a few times and tie an overhand knot in the wire.

2 String one end through three beads so there is one wire end on the top and one wire end on the bottom of the star. Place the star flat on the table and pull the wires straight up.

3 Thread both wires through a 10mm flower or rondelle bead **D**. Separate the wires and string each wire through a spike bead **E**, coming from different directions so they cross inside the spike.

4 Wrap the ends under the star and back up around, anchoring the wire around the base of the 10mm flower or rondelle bead **F**.

5 Repeat steps 3 and 4, reinforcing the wires through the spike bead one or two more times. Then bend the wire down below the star and run each wire through one of the holes in the button base **G**. Tie a last overhand knot to secure any extra wires. Do not trim the wires.

6 Make a second star with five points.

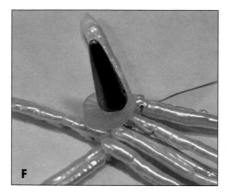

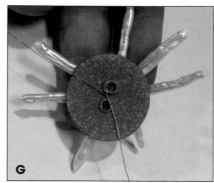

Step-by-step

1 Cut the cording to the length that you like for a necklace, taking into consideration that you need an extra 1½ in. on each side to fold over and secure the ends. The ends will naturally fray.

2 Tear two pieces of heavy-duty tape, each measuring 2–3 in. x ½ in. wide. Neatly wrap the frayed ends of the cording with this tape **H**.

3 Fold one end of the cord through an oval or donut and secure by wrapping a piece of 22-gauge wire in a freeform fashion around the adjacent cord pieces to secure. You do not have to knot the wire; just make sure it is wrapped firmly. Trim any extra wire **I**.

4 Wrap the bullion trim around the wire until it's covered. This can also be done in a freeform way. To knot the end of it, tie an overhand knot and use the precision scissors to trim it neatly **J**.

5 Repeat steps 3 and 4 on the other end.

6 Connect a toggle bar to one oval shell. Use the remaining oval shell as the toggle loop.

7 Using an overhand stitch, secure the sea star to the cording **K**, wrapping it around and tightly under the button base several times. Tie one last overhand knot to secure any extra wires. Trim the wires neatly. Repeat with the remaining star.

Another way to finish off a fiber cord wrapped through a donut-style terminator is to use tape or adhesive to secure the cording, and then a jewelry finding to cover up the end.

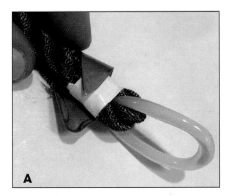

1 Fold cording through the donut ending or terminator.

2 Cut a ½-in. wide piece of tape, and wrap the adjacent cord pieces together so they are secure and tight. If you need to, tighten and add security with an additional piece of wire, wrapped tightly around the tape.

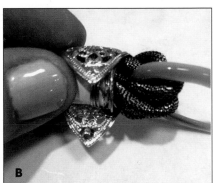

3 Using an oval or rectangle metal blank or filigree and rubber-coated pliers, fold the metal ends over the tape in a freeform but secure fashion, tightening any sharp or loose edges as you go **A**, **B**. Now you have a firmly secured loop at the end of your necklace, but the securing tape is covered.

harvested
elements
collage necklace

This project by Wendy Baker calls for a double set of skills to complete. Each half is easy to do and offers great design flexibility. First, build a base necklace, which can be worn alone or with added charms, and then cull through jewelry bits and pieces to build the detailed elements and dangles to embellish the base necklace.

materials

- mixed jewelry: clip-on earrings, screw-back earrings, mixed beads, bead caps, filigree, and charms This is the most flexible and exciting part of the vocabulary for your design.
- **45–85** mixed 6–8mm beads for the base necklace
- bead caps, mixed styles
- seed beads to offer a glint of color between the main beads and serve as spacing elements
- **30–50** 20-gauge jump rings in a variety of sizes
- **50** (approx.) headpins, in a metal to match your color scheme
- clasp
- flexible beading wire
- optional: 18-gauge wire in a metal to match your color scheme
- **8** crimp beads

tools

- pliers: flatnose, roundnose, crimping pliers, and a second pair of flatnose or chainnose pliers
- wire cutters
- small needle files: to smooth away any snags or rough spots
- clear fast-drying extra-hard nail polish for quick cosmetic touch-ups
- jewelry-grade glue just in case something needs a little extra confidence

DESIGN TIP! Instead of stringing my beads on flexible beading wire, I made loop components using 18-gauge wire and then linked them into the base necklace.

℮lement 1 the base necklace

1 Cut two 24-in. lengths of flexible beading wire (this will make a choker-length necklace with a little room to spare).

TIP! It is a lot easier to have more beading wire to finish the base necklace with than to struggle with some tiny ends. The wasted length of cable costs less in the long run than spending a lot of time trying to make something work.

2 On one wire, string two crimp beads and 1¼ in. of seed beads. With the wire end, go back through the crimp beads to form a beaded loop. Crimp the crimp beads.

3 Repeat step 2 with the remaining wire. You will string your base necklace with both of these pieces of wire simultaneously.

4 Holding both strands and loops together, start the base necklace. String a bead cap, a larger bead, a bead cap, a closed jump ring, and a seed bead. String a bead cap, a smaller bead, a bead cap, and a seed bead. Continue stringing beads in a pleasing pattern for 16–20 in., depending on your preference. The seed beads act as ball bearings between the larger beads, helping with flexibility. The closed jump rings become a method to attach charms to the necklace in the second phase of this design.

5 End the necklace with a bead cap. Separate the wires and string two crimp beads on each strand. String 1¼ in. of seed beads on each end. As in step 2, with each wire, go back through the crimp beads, creating a beaded loop. Double-check the tension of the necklace to avoid slack or too much tightness. You want a somewhat flexible expression, but no gaps between the beads. When the necklace looks good and you feel on top of the world, crimp the crimp beads one at a time and trim the extra wire close to the bead.

6 Attach a jump ring on one end of the necklace through both loops. Repeat on the other end. These will be used to attach a clasp to the necklace. if a lobster claw clasp is used, add a length of chain to the opposite end from the clasp to provide length adjustment.

⊖lement 2 the collage components

1 Gather your twinkling jewelry, components, and charms. Use a muffin tin or other segmented tray or box and sort the jewelry by size, shape, and/or color **A, B**.

2 Place the base necklace on a piece of plain paper. Using a tape measure or ruler, find the center (or the space closest to the center) of the necklace.

3 Now it's time to take the special things out of the tin and arrange them. Begin with a linear layout of pieces that look good to you. Add more for a fuller look or remove some for a more restrained look **C**.

4 Follow the directions in building blocks (p. 26) to make your repurposed pieces ready for attachment.

5 Make flower stacks, as in building blocks (p. 16). Vary the sizes and the shapes of the layers **D–H**.

6 Make charms from headpins, mixed beads, and bead caps. Make a wrapped loop above the beads. Making these is addictive and fun—no two need ever be the same. Use your original palette or begin a secondary one. Keep any leftovers for future projects. Insert these dangles among other prepared elements.

Step-by-step

As you work, a rhythm will emerge based on your original layout. Experiment with positioning the elements and the dangles. At this point, it is easiest to make changes and notes about them.

1 Open the jump ring at the center of the necklace and attach the middle/focal piece. You may need two jump rings straddling a center bead to get it to hang straight. Proper hanging is a very good thing. It will inform how other pieces may follow suit.

2 Add the other prepared parts. At this point, your notes might be useful as references while you have the necklace under construction in your hands.

3 If you have selected a lobster claw clasp for your closure, add a charm to the blank spot created by the chain end jump ring. It is a nice flourish and a finishing touch for the end of the piece.

Do a little jig to celebrate. You are done!

TIP! Since the first half of construction is a complete unit, you may feel like trying on the necklace as you go. This is a good exercise to check whether the piece is hanging nicely and if any areas need more work. Check to see if filing is needed anywhere. Double-check the jump rings for a full, seamless closure.

You can come up with alternative looks to this same design by using non-floral components, changing up color palettes, or harvesting different styles of vintage components.

TIDBIT! Wendy Baker is an über-talented, Providence, R. I.-based artist whose original work is also reminiscent of some designers of the past who put much time, effort, and craftsmanship into building their elements.

the
Tudors'
necklace

It's time to jump into stitching. Traditional and freeform embroidery stitches create layers and surface embellishments with loops and knots. Work up a version of each element first, and then decide how you want each positioned in the necklace. Or, plan the necklace and then work on the embellishments. Either way, I hope to inspire you to make a rich and deeply adorned piece, fit for royalty.

materials

- **3** 50–60mm Lucite filigree pieces
- 40–45mm stamping or metal component, donut shaped
- Swarovski sew-on crystals:
  - 20mm two-hole rectangle
  - **3** 15mm two-hole rectangles
  - 9mm two-hole oval
  - 18mm two-hole rectangle
- **30** 4mm faceted beads
- **6** side-drilled keshi pearls
- **9** spike beads
- 10mm metal square washer bead
- 8mm Czech glass bead
- 4–6mm Czech glass bead
- heishi or flat spacer
- 5g 8º seed beads
- **4–6** 6mm jump rings
- 20-gauge headpin
- 2–3 yds. 28-gauge wire
- 24 in. long-and-short link chain

tools

- Xuron precision scissors
- chainnose pliers

element 1 the filigree

1 The golden olive filigree in this necklace is the simplest in design. Anchor the center 18mm rectangle sew-on in the same way you would stitch a button onto a shirt: Wrap the brass wire a few times through the center hole in the filigree and around the edge. Sew through the first set of holes in the crystals. Wrap and anchor the crystal to the filigree base using a simple stitch. Continue in and out of the crystal and the filigree a few times. Repeat with the remaining hole. Finish by lashing the wire underneath the stitches you have already made. Trim any excess wire. Repeat to attach the 9mm oval to an edge **A**.

2 The orange filigree is just a little more complex. Anchor three 15mm sew-on crystals to the edges of the filigree, using the same technique as step 1 **B**. Anchor three spikes in the spaces between the crystals. Create a stack on a headpin with the 4mm Czech bead, the 8mm, and a square washer bead. String the stack through the center of the filigree, add a heishi or flat spacer, and secure with a small loop at the end of the headpin. Trim any extra wire.

3 The cranberry-colored piece in this necklace is the most highly adorned element of the necklace.

a. Stitch the 20mm rectangle to the center of the filigree as you did in step 1. Trim the wire end.

b. Stitch a spike to an edge of the filigree. Anchor tightly and trim the wires close. Repeat to stitch a total of six spikes with equal space between.

c. Using a running and sort of freeform stitch, add the seed beads and pearls. Begin with three 8º seed beads, lash the beads to the filigree, and then start stitching around the filigree. The process becomes intuitive. Add a few beads, stitch to an appropriate place to anchor, and then lash the wire around the filigree. Add a few more beads, stitch, and reinforce. When you come to a spike, add 12–14 8ºs and wrap a circle around the spike for a cool bezel-type look. Reinforce these loops with a stitch or two of raw wire to anchor them to the filigree. In the spaces between the spikes, add the pearls. Continue until you have covered the entire edge. As always, be sure to reinforce with extra stitches where necessary, and trim the wires.

element 2 the unchained link

1 This link is made with 4mm faceted beads sewn in a simple peyote stitch—see "weaving chain links" (p. 22). Make it as narrow or thick as you'd like. Mine is only two rows and just hints at a woven look. You could certainly make a wider chain link using more beads and more rows. String the first row of beads and then loop through the vintage donut shaped piece and the orange filigree. Continue stitching in peyote until the link is the desired size. Connect the two ends of the peyote strip **C**.

Step-by-step

1 Arrange the elements until you have a pleasing design.

2 Connect the elements with jump rings. If desired, use a small segment of chain between two elements for an asymmetrical look.

3 Connect each end of the centerpiece to a chain link. Choose a length that's long enough to slip on over your head, or if you'd like, cut the chain in equal pieces and attach a clasp to each end.

TIP! Be sure to adjust where the pieces are linked together with jump rings so that the elements hang straight.

Miriam's
ladder
pendant

The first piece of jewelry I ever designed that was inspired by Miriam Haskell is the one you see on p. 69. It's built using a series of wires and pins that are coated with pearls and linked together to establish a base. The base is wired with some stacked and stitched components. Miriam's Ladder pendant is a simplified take on that style. You can play with this piece using various materials to create totally different looks while practicing the same technique.

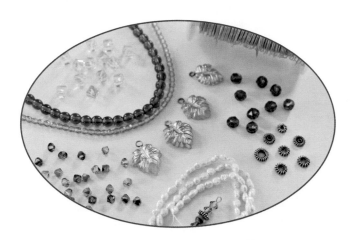

materials

- **88–110** 4mm assorted beads: bicone crystals, fire-polished beads, rounds, and others
- **10–20** 4–5mm silver flat beads
- **24** 6mm assorted beads: crystals and freshwater pearls
- **4** 14mm charms or pendants
- chain
- clasp
- **6** 2-in. headpins
- **20** 2-in. eyepins (or a spool of 22-gauge wire)
- 30 in. 28-gauge brass wire

tools

- roundnose pliers
- wire cutters
- Xuron precision scissors

⊖lement 1 the pendant

1 String six 4mm beads onto an eyepin. Trim the end of the eyepin to ¼ in. Make a plain loop parallel to the loop at the other end. Repeat to make a total of four beaded eyepins.

2 On an eyepin, string a 4mm bead, the eye of a beaded eyepin, a 4mm, a beaded eyepin, a 4mm, a beaded eyepin, a 4mm, a beaded eyepin and a 4mm for a total of five beads interspersed with four eyepins.

TIP! Intersperse silver rondelles with the 4mm beads as long as they don't add to the length of your link.

3 Using chainnose pliers, secure all the plain loops.

4 String a 4mm bead on an eyepin. String through the eye of the pin at the bottom left of the unit you've just made. String a 4mm, an plain eyepin, and the next eye. Repeat until you have strung the last eye and a 4mm. Finish by trimming the wire to ¼ in. and making a plain loop at the end. You should have a new section of four dangling eyepins.

5 Repeat step 1 on the dangling eyepins.

6 Repeat steps 3 and 4.

7 Repeat step 1 on the dangling eyepins. Repeat step 4 but omit the new eyepins.

8 Open the loop of an eyepin and string a charm. Close the loop. String a 4mm, a spacer, and a 4mm. Make a plain loop at the end. Connect the loop to a loop at the bottom edge of the pendant. Repeat three times for a total of four dangles.

9 Cut a 24-in. piece of wire. Starting at the upper corner of the pendant, secure the wire with a couple of overhand wraps between the top two 4mm beads. Add a 6mm bead and lash the wire to the next 4mm bead along the side of the pendant. It's OK to skip a bead if you get a better position and neater wraps.

10 Continue working as in step 9 until you reach the bottom edge of the pendant. Secure the last bead by tying an overhand knot and wrapping the wire around the 4mm beads a few times. Neatly trim the wire ends.

11 Repeat steps 9 and 10 on the other edge.

12 String a 6mm crystal on a headpin. Make a wrapped loop above the bead. Repeat to make a total of six dangles.

13 Open a loop at the end of a horizontal eyepin. Attach the dangle and close the loop. Repeat to attach a dangle to each horizontal loop.

Step-by-step

1 Open a loop on the top edge of the pendant with chainnose pliers. Connect it to a chain link, closing securely with pliers.

2 Repeat step 1 on the other edge of the pendant and with the other end of the chain.

3 If desired, cut the chain in half and attach a clasp half to each end.

TIP! Instead of using chain, hang the pendant from a fine ribbon, a fun cord, or a beaded necklace.

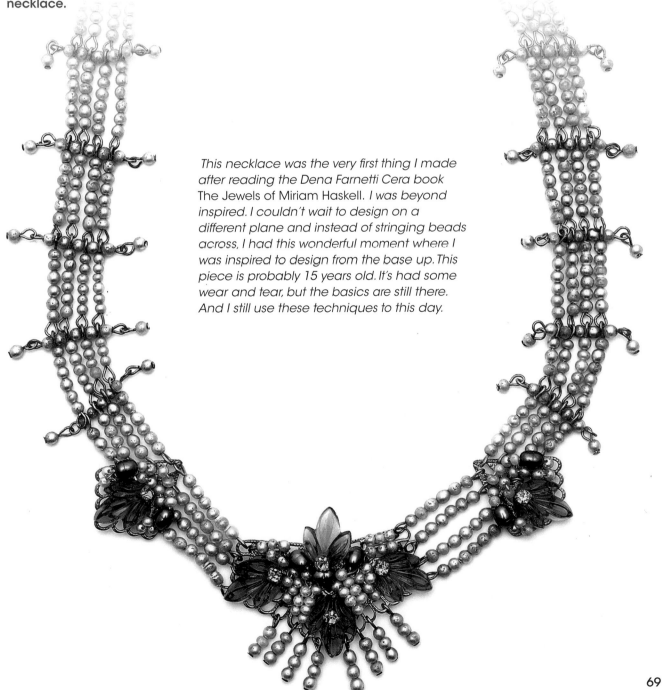

This necklace was the very first thing I made after reading the Dena Farnetti Cera book The Jewels of Miriam Haskell. *I was beyond inspired. I couldn't wait to design on a different plane and instead of stringing beads across, I had this wonderful moment where I was inspired to design from the base up. This piece is probably 15 years old. It's had some wear and tear, but the basics are still there. And I still use these techniques to this day.*

wrapped in chain
necklace

I love the look of a sculptured shape covered by beads. Haskell did this technique superbly well. In addition to chain, try covering any surface: sprockets, bike parts, found objects, shells, and glass shards—anything you find that you wish to cover. All you need to do is use this beyond-easy technique called lashing. We'll get some practice in this project.

materials

- 20 in. carved wooden chain
- **600** 3x4mm faceted rondelles in two or three colors
- 20–30 ft. 28-gauge brass wire
- 15 in. silk or other ribbon, optional
- **4** crimp beads, optional
- 11º seed beads, optional
- slide clasp, optional

tools

- Xuron precision scissors
- chainnose pliers

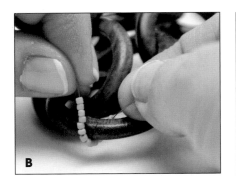

Step-by-step

1 Cut a 20-in. piece of wire. Anchor the wire on a chain link. String five faceted rondelles. Using the lashing technique (p. 21), start to wrap and lash a beaded chain link **A–D**.

2 As you run out of wire, reinforce the stitching by backtracking through a few beads and knotting the wire a few times around an anchored wrap **E**. Anchor a new wire and continue lashing until the chain link is covered as you like **F**.

3 Wrap several chain links with beads. I cover about one-fourth and leave three-fourths exposed, both for aesthetic reasons and so the links lie nicely next to each other.

4 Optional closure: String 12 rondelles and a crimp bead. Loop the rondelles through an end chain link. Go back through the crimp bead and crimp. String about 3 in. of rondelles and a crimp bead. String 12 11ºs and half a clasp. Go back through the crimp bead. Pull the wire ends tight and crimp the crimp bead. Trim the wire. Repeat on the other end of the necklace with the remaining clasp half.

5 Optional closure: Cut the ribbon to the desired length for finishing the necklace. Loop one end through an end chain link. Freeform wire-wrap the ribbon and tail together, using fine brass wire. Repeat on the other end.

cuties
necklace

I love to build beads or create components from beads that would have otherwise looked totally different if strung merely through their own holes. I have this habit of making what I call "cuties." They are simply a component built of beads, similar to a beaded bead, but easier to build and sculpt. You'll learn how to make these and use them to add dimension to a strung necklace.

materials

- **30** 14–16mm Lucite beads in several shapes
- **16** 4–6mm sew-on or disk beads
- **24** top-drilled drop beads
- **24** petal beads
- **16** 4mm rondelles
- **2** crimp beads
- 16 ft. 26-gauge brass wire
- 2 ft. elastic cord

tools

- Xuron precision scissors

⊖lement 1 the cuties

Make three drop-bead and three four-petal bead cuties using the Cluster Cuties technique (p. 23).

⊖tep-by-step

1 Cut 2 ft. of elastic cord. Center a drop-bead cutie on the cord.

2 On each end, string three Lucite beads.

3 On each end, string a petal cutie and three Lucite beads.

4 On each end, string a drop cutie, two Lucite beads, a petal cutie, and three Lucite beads.

5 On each end, string four Lucite beads. Check the fit, and add or remove Lucite beads from each end if necessary.

6 Tie a surgeon's knot and hide the knot in a bead.

alternative project

unchained
necklace

One of the elements of Haskell jewelry that I've always loved is the way something functional is built out of what is commonly considered purely decorative— such as beads. For example, a signature look is to create a chain out of simply stringing beads together into links. It's so beyond simple, but the technique becomes a very powerful design element.

materials

- assortment of teensies
- 14 in. chain
- link or focal bead made into a link
- pendant
- 28-gauge brass wire
- clasp, optional
- **2** jump rings, optional

tools

- wire cutters
- Xuron precision scissors
- chainnose pliers

Element 1 the unchained segment

1 Cut a 6-in. piece of wire.

2 String 10–12 teensies. Tie a square knot to complete a circle of beads and string each wire end back through a few beads on each side in opposite directions **A**. Trim the wire.

3 Cut a 6-in. piece of wire. String 10–12 teensies and the link you just created **B**. Finish it using the same knot-and-trim technique as in step 2.

4 Repeat step 3 until you have reached the desired length of your unchained segment.

Step-by-step

1 Create a single unchained link and use it to connect the unchained element to the pendant on one side.

2 Create a single unchained link to connect a 2-in. piece of chain to the other side of the pendant.

3 Make a single unchained link, and use it to connect the 2-in. chain to the link component. Repeat on the other side of the component and connect to a 12-in. piece of chain.

4 Create a last single unchained link and connect the end of the 12-in. chain to your initial length of unchained links.

5 Add a clasp if desired in the back of the necklace: Cut the traditional chain in center of the back of the necklace. Connect a clasp half to each end.

alternative project

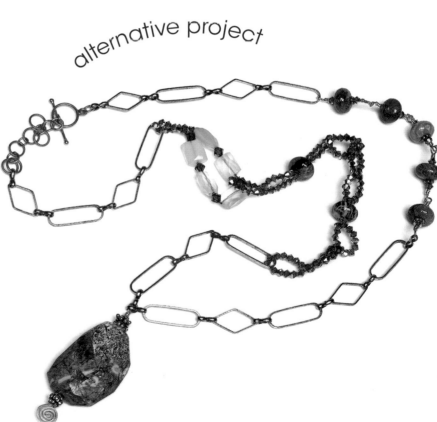

nouveau
cluster clasp
necklace

While this amazing Bakelite pendant might be the star of this show, achieve this look with any favorite pendant or focal drop piece. The other star might just be the clasp, ornately stitched with various materials. Mesh bases mean you can turn plain findings into fabulous focals. Imagine how you can combine form and function in interesting ways! You'll learn stitching techniques in this project along with finishing techniques for hiding freeform wiring.

materials

- mesh dome box clasp
- 18–24 in. fine chain
- 25–30mm top-drilled drop bead
- 35–45mm drop pendant
- assortment of 3mm–10mm decorative shell beads
- **2 or more** 4–6mm disk beads
- assortment of teensies
- 3–4 ft. 28-gauge brass wire
- **4** 4mm jump rings

tools

- chainnose pliers
- wire cutters
- Xuron precision scissors

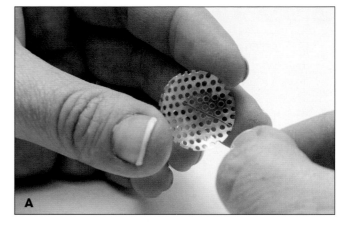

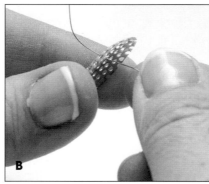

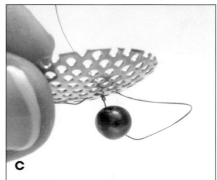

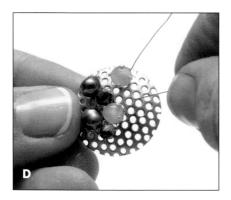

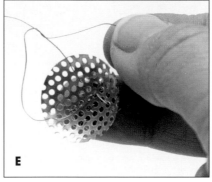

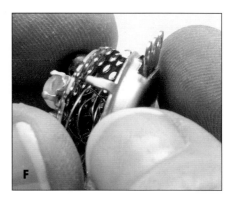

TIP! I like the look of exposed wire, so I placed a few extra stitches around the surfaces of the larger beads. Not only is this nice aesthetically, it adds to the sturdiness of the stitching.

⊙lement 1 the embellished clasp

1 Remove the mesh dome from the clasp **A**.

2 Cut 24 in. of wire. Anchor the wire through two holes in the mesh **B**, wrapping a few times to reinforce it. Tie a knot in one wire end.

3 String one larger or a few smaller beads and stitch down through another hole in the mesh **C**. Stitch back up through the closest hole to your last stitch.

4 Repeat step 2, stitching in a freeform pattern and anchoring each stitch with an extra stitch or a knot as you go **D**.

5 When you are finished or if you run out of wire, make an extra wrap and a knot **E**. Then trim the wire neatly. Repeat step 1 to add more wire.

6 Replace the embellished dome on the clasp back **F**.

Element 2 dangles and drops

1 String the 25mm drop on a 9-in. length of wire and leave a 3-in. tail. Make a set of wraps above the bead.

2 Make a wrapped loop above the wraps.

3 Wrap the tail beyond the original wraps and around the bead, covering about ¼ in. of the tip.

4 String a disk bead onto a headpin and make a plain loop above the bead.

TIDBIT! During WWI and WWII, metals became hard to source since they were being used for artillery. Jewelry designers began to turn to naturals and plastics in the place of brass, copper, and even silver.

A

Step-by-step

1 String the large pendant on the chain.

2 Cut a 1-ft. piece of wire. String a chain link above the pendant, a disk bead, and a chain link on the other side of the pendant. Pull the wire tight and stitch through the chain and disk bead again. Make decorative wraps across the surface of the bead. Tie one overhand knot to secure the wraps and then trim the extra wire **A**.

3 Use jump rings to attach a chain end to the center loop of one half of the clasp. Repeat with the other clasp half.

4 Use jump rings to attach the wrapped drop bead and the disk-bead dangle to the remaining loops in the three-strand clasp **B**.

B

TIP! If your box clasp doesn't have a removable back, use extra-fine tweezer-nosed pliers to really get in there and pull your stitches through.

silver lining
necklace

This necklace features several of my favorite old-time vintage jewelry design techniques: an adorned piece of filigree layered on a pendant, a bead-wrapped bead, and a filigree decorated clasp—all in one piece. This project is a good example of how you can use older methods with modern materials for a fresh look. This seemingly simple piece combines many of the building blocks learned in this book.

materials

- **2** shell donuts sized so one can lie inside the other
- ornate metal filigree
- **4** strands of teensies
- **3** 14mm carved shell center-hole flower beads
- **6** 12mm carved shell center-hole flower beads
- **11** 7mm carved shell center-hole flower beads
- 18–22mm Lucite bead
- 3-strand screen clasp
- flexible beading wire
- **6** crimp beads
- 28-gauge brass wire
- 12 in. 22-gauge sterling silver or silver-plated wire

tools

- Xuron precision scissors
- roundnose pliers
- crimping pliers
- rubber-coated pliers

Element 1 stitched clasp

Remove the screen from the prong setting (if necessary). Using basic stitching from the building blocks (p. 19), anchor the fine brass wire and begin stitching sterling silver teensies and center-hole carved flowers to the screen, making sure to reinforce the anchors when larger beads are added. Leave a border of unstitched space around the screen. Once you have finished stitching and adorning the screen, set the screen into the prong setting of the clasp using rubber coated pliers.

Element 2 wrapped bead

1 Cut 1–2 yds. (a comfortable length) of 28-gauge brass wire. String the Lucite bead, leaving a 1-ft. tail.

2 Pick up as many teensies as will wrap around half the bead, and bring the wire back through the hole exiting with the tail. Pick up the same number of teensies and come back through the bead.

3 To add a flower, pick up two fewer than half the number of teensies strung in step 1. String a flower from back to front. String three teensies as an anchor or stamen. Go back through the center hole of the flower, exiting the back. String two fewer than half the number of teensies strung in step 1. Wrap the wire through the bead. When you are finished wrapping the bead, secure the tails by wrapping and looping or knotting reinforcements underneath the already-secured wraps. Nestle and hide the wire in the beads.

4 Repeat steps 2 and 3 until you have the desired number of wraps around the bead.

Element 3 filigree dangle

Using the stitching technique (p. 19), adorn a filigree piece using six 7mm and two 12mm carved shell flowers. Leave the very top of the component unadorned, as you will use this space later to anchor the dangle to the smaller of the two donuts and the necklace itself.

Step-by-step

side one

1 Cut a 30-in. length of beading wire. Crimp one end of the wire to one loop of the clasp. String three rondelles and 6 in. of teensies. String two rondelles. String 1–1½ in. of teensies (enough to comfortably wrap around the larger donut). Wrap the strand around the large donut and go back through the two rondelles. String 6 in. of teensies, three rondelles, a crimp bead, and the middle clasp loop. Go back through the crimp bead and crimp. Trim the excess wire.

2 Cut a 30-in. piece of beading wire. Do not crimp it to the clasp. As in step 1, string beads to reach the donut, beginning with three rondelles and continuing with teensies. End with two rondelles. String the same amount of beads to comfortably wrap the large donut as in step 1. String back through the rondelles and string back through the beads strung in the beginning of this step. String a crimp bead over both wire ends and string the remaining clasp loop. Go back through the crimp bead and crimp. Trim the excess wire.

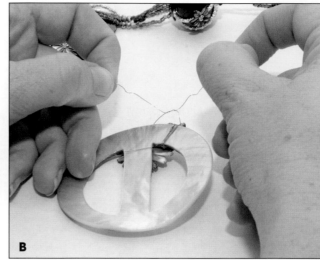

side two

3 Cut a 30-in. piece of beading wire. Crimp one end to an end loop of the clasp. String two rondelles and 4½ in. of teensies. String a 14mm carved shell flower bead, the wrapped Lucite bead, and a 14mm carved shell flower bead. String 1 in. of teensies and two rondelles. String 1–1½ in. of teensies (enough to comfortably wrap around the larger donut). Wrap the strand around the donut and then and go back through the two rondelles. String 1 in. of beads, go through the wrapped Lucite bead, and string another 4½ in. of beads. String a crimp bead and the middle loop of the clasp. Go back through the crimp bead, crimp, and trim the excess wire.

4 Repeat step 2, passing through the wrapped Lucite bead as you string back through the strand.

5 Cut a 24-in. piece of fine brass wire. Make two wraps around the donut, to the right of where the necklace is anchored. Reinforce by passing the wire under itself and tying a knot. Pick up a 12mm carved shell flower bead. String three teensies **A**. Go back through the center hole of the flower bead and exit the bead. Wrap the wire around the donut twice, pressing down on the flower so it lies flat and is centered on the donut. Pick up a 7mm carved shell flower bead, three teensies, and then go back through the flower bead, exiting the back. Wrap the wire twice around the donut, making sure that the flower lies where you'd like it. Repeat with the 6mm and the 14mm carved shell flowers. Reinforce with two or three more wraps underneath the flower beads. Pass the wire underneath the wraps and make a couple of knots as you go **B**. Trim the ends of the wire neatly.

6 Use chainnose pliers to wrap a tiny spiral or loop on the end of the 12-in. piece of 22-gauge silver wire. String through a 7mm carved flower and the top empty space of the metal filigree component. If the donut has a hole, string the wire through the donut. (If the donut does not have a hole, use an 18-in. piece of wire and wrap it around the donut to attach the filigree to the front.) Make a wire-wrapped loop on the back of the pendant and trim.

7 Cut a 12–15-in. length of the 28-gauge brass wire. String 1 in. of teensies mixed with a few rondelles. String the pendant through the wire-wrapped loop you made in step 6. Add more teensies and rondelles and wrap the wire around the larger donut, between where the necklace is anchored on each side, centering it in the necklace. Wrap the wire back through the beads and the pendant to reinforce. (The more times that the fine brass wire goes through the pendant and the beads, the better.) Repeat this step 2–3 times, reinforcing through each a few times. Neatly trim the wire ends after you have knotted under the wire wraps a few times.

free-for-all hoop
earrings

These hoops are a modern-day spin on a freeform covered surface. While much stitching in older vintage jewelry was very deliberate and neat, there were times when freeform stitching covered surface areas. In this project, we'll use that technique to cover the base of a hoop to create a sculpted surface adornment.

materials

- pair of metal earring hoops
- **2** ½–1 in. drop or focal beads
- **200–300** 2–3mm glass beads or seed beads
- **4** 5mm rose montées or 4mm glass beads
- 28-gauge brass wire

tools

- chainnose pliers
- Xuron precision scissors

TIP! This is a great project to repurpose your old boring hoop earrings. Check thrift shops and yard sales and look for crazy metal hoops in gauges like 18–12-gauge. Look for some that are sturdier than the classic wire hoops you find at bead stores.

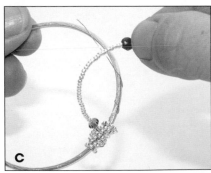

⑤tep-by-step

1 Cut a 30-in. length of brass wire. Loosely fold in half and wrap a few times around the hoop **A**.

2 String a few 2–3mm or seed beads and wrap the beaded wire around the hoop **B**.

3 String a 4mm bead, more seed beads and a 4mm **C**. Wrap the beaded wire around the hoop **D**.

4 Work until you've covered about half of the area. String a focal bead and a few more 2–3mms or seed beads and wrap the beaded wire around the hoop.

5 Continue beading on the other side of the focal, creating a sculpted area that is the mirror image of the first **E**. Wrap the wire tail around the hoop to anchor the wire and go back through a few beads **F**. Trim the wire tail **G**.

TIDBIT! What is a rose montée? Rose montée refers to a bead that has been most commonly used in garment and fabric embellishment throughout history. They are typically made of a metal base and have a crystal or glass stone set into them. There are usually two holes in a diagonal pattern in the metal on the back, so they are easy to anchor and stitch to garments. They are a great component to use in freeform beadweaving.

alternative project

⑤tep-by-step

1 Cut a 30-in. length of brass wire. Loosely fold in half. String a drop bead.

2 String two 2–3mm glass beads, a disk bead or rose montée, and two glass beads. String each wire end back through the hole in the drop bead in opposite directions. String two glass beads, a disk bead or rose montée, and two glass beads.

Wrap to the other side of the drop bead and thread both wires back through the hole in the drop bead.

3 You now should have two wire ends, each coming out one side of the pendant, along with some pretty little visual elements on either side of the tip of your drop bead. Wrap both wire ends around the center of the hoop earring a few times, lashing and knotting to reinforce as you go.

4 Once the beaded wire has been secured to the hoop, separate the wire ends. Work one side of the pendant at a time. Add 4–6 glass beads, wrap around the hoop, then lash the wire. Add more beads, and make another lash around the hoop. Repeat this until you have the look you want. Wrap and lash the remaining wire to anchor and trim.

5 Repeat step 4 on the other side of the pendant.

6 Make a second earring.

down by the sea
stitched cuff

I love the simplicity and even more, the sentiment of this piece. I live on the coast of Maine. My family has a lovely camp on the ocean where my kids can spend their weekend summer days digging through tide pools, running in the sand, and skipping rocks across the waves. Me? I'm combing the beaches, head down, looking for treasures. My current favorites to hunt are sea glass and old aluminum can tops that have aged. This piece is inspired by my summertime surroundings. In this project, we'll work with eyelets to create a functional ajoure out of a cuff bracelet.

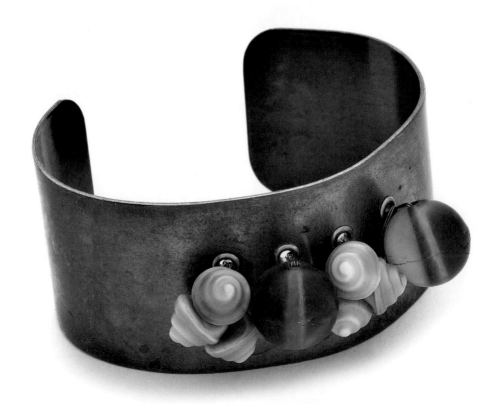

materials
- copper cuff (or make your own using sheet)
- **8** ³⁄₃₂-in. diameter, ³⁄₃₂-in. long brass or copper eyelets
- **2** 10–15mm frosted glass rounds
- **6** 6mm glass seashell beads
- 24–36 in. 28-gauge brass wire

tools
- chasing hammer
- Crafted Findings tool and vise
- bench block
- letter stamps
- polishing pads
- permanent marker

element 1
the cuff bracelet

1 Use the Crafted Findings tool to pierce two rows of four ³⁄₃₂-in. diameter holes **A**.

2 Stamp the edge by turning the cuff over and setting it on the bench block. Use a marker to mark where you want the letters. My cuff reads "Down by the Sea." Stamp each letter with the chasing hammer, striving for one firm strike. Color letters in with the marker and once dry, polish off excess ink with the polish pads.

3 Set an eyelet in each hole using the eyelet flaring attachment for the Crafted Findings tool **B**.

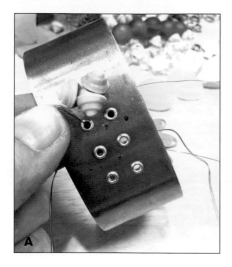

Step-by-step

1 Cut a comfortable length of wire. I like to use about 24 in. If necessary, you can always add extra.

2 Anchor the wire by stitching it up and around the two end eyelet holes.

3 Bring the wire from back to front through one of the end eyelets. String a cluster of three seashell beads. Sew the wire down through the eyelet hole on the upper row, top left. Reinforce the beads by sewing through the same holes and beads two to three times. Then sew up through the next eyelet on the bottom row **A**.

4 String a frosted round bead. Sew through the adjacent eyelet. Secure the bead in its place by sewing through the same loops and bead two to three times.

5 Repeat steps 3 and 4 to finish the remaining rows of beads. Once you have anchored the last frosted bead, add extra security by sewing the wire under the last stitches, and making a knot behind the cuff a few times. Trim the wire neatly.

alternative project: hammered dragonfly bracelet

The same eyelet-setting technique can be used to attach just one plain bead to a surface, or as a base for loads of adornment. This piece is a perfect example of how eyelets can create unique bases from once simple blanks.

mod stitched
hoop earrings

Oh so retro. These hoops are just a fun way to showcase how to create a custom ajoure component for jewelry making. Find hoops in thrift shops or departments stores made from different materials to achieve varied looks to this project. See the drilling building blocks (p. 24) for details on how to drill and make your own ajoure.

materials

- pair of vintage Lucite earrings (or any drillable material with some surface area)
- assorted teensies
- 6 ft. 28-gauge brass wire

tools

- Xuron precision scissors
- rotary tool with fine bits
- drilling setup: tray with water, wooden base, eye protection
- permanent marker

Element 1 custom ajoure

1 Use a marker to indicate where you'd like your stitches to be on the hoops. Use the rotary tool to drill holes to create your own base or ajoure components **A**, **B**.

alternative project

This pair of earrings was made in the same way as the others in this project; however, they show how a different look can be accomplished when just the surface is adorned instead of wrapping the entire body of the hoop.

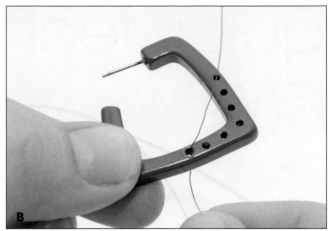

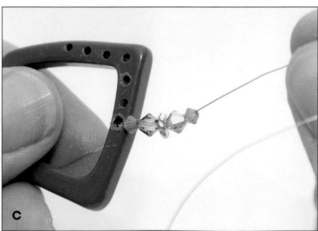

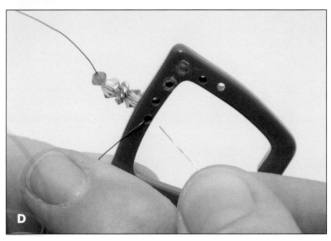

Step-by-step

1 Cut a 24–30-in. piece of wire **A**.

2 Center the wire through a hole and anchor the wire **B**. You'll work the earring alternating from one side to another, using half the wire at a time and crossing the wires so they are always changing sides.

3 String two to three teensies on one wire end and stitch through the next hole **C, D**. Repeat with the other wire end, stitching the wire through the same, or a close by, hole in the opposite direction. This way you should still have a wire coming out of each side of the hoop.

4 Repeat step 3 in a freeform fashion. You will be covering the surface area of the hoops as you go and always trading the sides you are working on. Be sure to take a stitch on each side, alternately, so you use the wire ends equally.

5 When the hoops are covered and you are happy with the look of the stitches and beading, anchor the wire by a making a few stitches through the holes in the hoop with just the wire. When you have anchored the wire and stitches, carefully trim the ends.

TIP! When you are finishing the earrings, hide the naked wire under the beads. Be careful and think through the placement of the stitches, choosing spots where the wire blends well with the beads.

quick technique review

wrapped loop

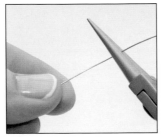

1 Grasp the wire 1½ in. from the end with roundnose pliers.

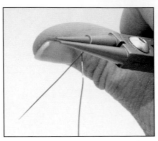

2 Bring the long end of the wire over the pliers' jaw until it crosses the tail.

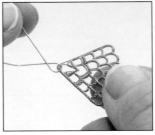

3 Remove the pliers and add the finding.

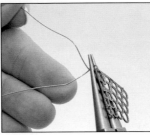

4 Position the jaws of the pliers across the loop to stabilize it.

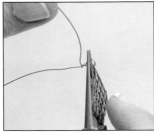

5 Hold the tail at the end, and wrap around the working wire.

6 Trim the wire tail and tuck the wraps.

wraps above a top-drilled bead

1 Center a top-drilled bead on a 3-in. piece of wire. Bend each wire upward to form a squared-off "U" shape.

2 Cross the wires into an "X" above the bead.

3 Using chainnose pliers, make a small bend in each wire so the ends form a right angle.

4 Wrap the horizontal wire around the vertical wire as in a wrapped loop. Trim the excess wire.

plain loop

1 Trim the wire or head pin ⅜ in. above the top bead. Make a right-angle bend close to the bead.

2 Grab the wire's tip with roundnose pliers. The tip of the wire should be flush with the pliers. Roll the wire to form a half circle. Release the wire.

3 Reposition the pliers in the loop and continue rolling.

4 The finished loop should form a centered circle above the bead.

crimping

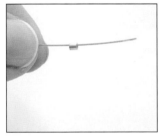

1 String a 2x2 tube crimp bead on flexible beading wire.

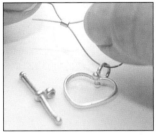

2 String a clasp half. Go back through the crimp bead.

3 Separate the wires to each side of the crimp, and using the part of the pliers that has the tooth fold the crimp in half.

4 Move to the next notch on the crimping pliers and position the crimp inside it. Then fold the crimp closed on itself. Use the needlenose on the end to secure the crimp if it needs any tightening.

opening and closing loops or jump rings

1 Hold the loop or jump ring with two pairs of chainnose pliers or chainnose and round-nose pliers, as shown.

2 To open the loop or jump ring, bring one pair of pliers toward you and push the other pair away. String materials on the open loop or jump ring. Reverse the steps to close the open loop or jump ring.

square knot

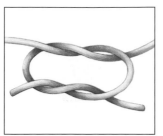

Bring the left-hand thread over the right-hand thread and around. Cross right over left, and go through the loop.

overhand knot

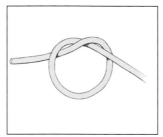

Make a loop and pass the working end through it. Pull the ends to tighten the knot.

acknowledgments

This book has been a long time in the making and I have had so much support and help from so many amazing people at each stage.

I have to first thank Karin Van Voorhees for making sense out of piles of jewelry, sometimes disjointed thoughts, incomplete directions and for basically being able to see my ideas through my own jumbled thoughts. (See…I just said "thoughts" twice.) Her clarity of vision, professionalism, and grace have made this process not only painless, but truly a fun project.

Jessica Lovendale is a goddess of photography. Her willingness to drive four states away to help me shoot these beautiful photographs (any of the less-than-beautiful photos are mine), not just once, but three times for four different photo sessions has been so appreciated. You all need to hire her—she's the next big thing in photography. She's amazing, smart, and a true talent.

Thanks go to Ashley Bunting and Wendy Baker for their generous additions to this book. They are both jewelry artisans whose work inspires me and takes my breath away every time I see something new. Huge "thank you's" to both of them.

My staff and co-workers at The Beadin' Path: not only as I've worked on this book, but those who have come before. Thank you all for your hard work, support, and ideas. I wouldn't have been able to put the time into this if it weren't for all you who have kept things running.

And huge props go to my great aunt Kay Bowker and my grandmothers, Marion Lovendale Cram and Gerry Parker, all of whom let me play in their jewelry boxes as a little girl and started me down the path of playing with and figuring out how to make trinkets.

Big thanks to my husband, Chris DeSimone, for his support and willingness to cook a lot more than usual throughout this book process. Love and thanks to my boys for their words of encouragement ("You're STILL working on that book, Mom?"), and for helping me pick up bead spills and stage photo setups when asked.

This book wouldn't be possible without the support of my mom and business partner in The Beadin' Path, Inc., Jan Parker. I feel so fortunate that I get to work alongside my mother and my friend on a daily basis, as I have for almost 20 years.

~~~~~~~~~~~~~~~~~~~~~~~~~~~~~~~~~~~

about the author

Heather DeSimone has been taking apart and putting together jewelry for 35 years. She lives in Maine with her husband, Chris, and her two boys Max and Alex. She has been co-owner of *The Beadin' Path* and *beadinpath.com* since 1993. Her jewelry line, *Leetie Lovendale,* can be found online as well as at markets and boutiques across the country. When she's not playing with jewelry parts, you can find her enjoying… ahh, she's always playing with jewelry parts.

Discover More
Jewelry Projects
to Make and Share!

Multistrand Jewelry

Master the challenges of multistrand jewelry! With a wide variety of projects from *Bead Style* magazine, a thorough Basics section, and detailed instructions, this book helps you solve the tricky problems of this popular style. Includes valuable tips on creating the right drape for necklaces, choosing the proper length for each strand, and working with cones, spacers, and multistrand clasps.

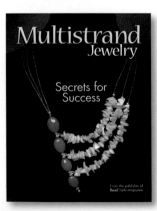

64513 • $17.95

Jewelry Projects from a Beading Insider

Cathy Jakicic knows firsthand what stumps beaders, what they're curious about, and what excites them.

She generously shares 150+ insider tips, tricks, and secrets to creating fun and wearable jewelry in this all-new collection of 30 original designs. She offers lots of options with project alternatives, matching accessories, and budget-friendly choices.

67026 • $19.95